PRAYER
WARRIOR

PRAYER WARRIORS

BY

STUART HOWELL
MILLER

alyson books
los angeles | new york

MANUFACTURED IN THE UNITED STATES OF AMERICA.

THIS TRADE PAPERBACK ORIGINAL IS PUBLISHED BY
ALYSON PUBLICATIONS INC.,
P.O. BOX 4371, LOS ANGELES, CALIFORNIA 90078-4371.
DISTRIBUTION IN THE UNITED KINGDOM BY
TURNAROUND PUBLISHER SERVICES LTD.,
UNIT 3 OLYMPIA TRADING ESTATE, COBURG ROAD, WOOD GREEN,
LONDON N22 6TZ ENGLAND.

FIRST EDITION: MAY 1999

03 02 01 00 99 🄰 10 9 8 7 6 5 4 3 2 1

ISBN 1-55583-445-0

LIBRARY OF CONGRESS CATALOGING-IN-PUBLICATION DATA
    MILLER, STUART HOWELL, 1965–
        PRAYER WARRIORS / BY STUART HOWELL MILLER.
        ISBN 1-55583-445-0
        1. MILLER, STUART HOWELL. 2. HOMOSEXUALITY—RELIGIOUS
ASPECTS—CHRISTIANITY—CASE STUDIES. 3. COMING OUT (SEXUAL
ORIENTATION)—UNITED STATES—CASE STUDIES. 4. GAYS—UNITED
STATES—FAMILY RELATIONSHIPS—CASE STUDIES. 5. FUNDAMEN-
TALISM—UNITED STATES—CASE STUDIES. 6. GAY MEN—UNITED
STATES—BIOGRAPHY. I. TITLE.
    BR115.H6M53 1999
    261.8'35766' 092—DC21
    [B]   98-55996 CIP

To Will

ACKNOWLEDGMENTS

There are so many people to thank—friends, coworkers, entire organizations—for helping to make this book a reality that I realized, when I started compiling a list, there would only be sufficient space to thank individuals substantially involved in helping produce the final product. To those who contributed but are not mentioned here, please know that my love, admiration, and gratitude lie within these pages and in my heart. I would like to specifically thank:

Laura Gross, my agent, for believing in this project from the beginning and for understanding that rewards come in many different packages.

Trent Duffy for help in getting me started with his incredible writing and editing skills and for helping me find the story inside me.

Nancy Lamb for her compassionate insight and her ability to transform a Southern boy's long-winded storytelling into something worth reading.

Greg Constante, Dan Cullinane, and the entire Alyson family for their hard work and belief in the book.

And Scott Brassart for 18 years of friendship and for making this all possible.

CHAPTER 1

THE HOME FRONT

August 1992

"Ladies and gentlemen, we are beginning our descent into Nashville. The captain has turned on the fasten seat belts sign. Would you please move your seat backs and tray tables into the..."

I zoned out on the flight attendant's spiel and exhaled deeply, excited and nervous about what lay ahead. Excited because this was my first trip home since moving to California at the beginning of spring. Nervous because it was finally time to tell my family I am gay.

Maybe my parents had already guessed my news, but I wanted them to know for certain. After five months away I needed to be honest with them about my life. A few years earlier I had been the closeted president of my college fraternity and had dated sorority girls. Now, at 26, I was comfortable with myself, my sexuality, and my job as an AIDS educator in Los Angeles. It was time to share the whole of my life with my family in Tennessee.

I swallowed hard as the flight attendants roamed the cabin making last-minute preparations. My seat mates, Victoria and Jane, smiled at me. Reassuring. Victoria oversaw the AIDS program at Meharie Medical Center. I had met her through the job I'd had in Nashville before moving to California. She and her lover had been at the same AIDS conference in Washington, D.C., that I'd just attended, and by coincidence we had all booked the same flight to Nashville.

At the conference I had told Victoria about my plan to come out to my family. Like everyone I had talked to, she encouraged me to take this important step. In Washington, and again on the plane, Victoria gave me hope, emphasizing how good her own coming-out experience had been.

I listened and told myself again and again, "This *is* the right thing to do. This *is* the right thing to do." All my friends said so. The available literature said so. *I* said so. It was time to end the years of deceit, lies, half-truths, hints, and manipulation. It was time to share my secret with my parents.

I was already out to all of my friends and was happier with my life than I had ever been. My homosexuality was hidden only from my family. My friends had reacted positively when I came out to them, but my parents were fundamentalist Christians—very different animals.

I knew my parents loved me, but I also knew their religious beliefs overshadowed everything else. In a letter I had received a few weeks earlier, my mother gave me news of my older brother and two younger sisters. Then, as if she intuitively knew of my desire to come out, she referred to a recent phone call in which I had told her about my new job:

> *I miss you and really have a lot of fear about your life and the friends you have. I know you think you are making a contribution where one is greatly needed, but I'm afraid you will be hurt in the process and that the people you have so much contact with are not a positive influence.*

My mother had been generally supportive of my work at Nashville Cares, the AIDS organization I worked for in Tennessee, but she disapproved of the people I worked with, of their "lifestyle." So when I moved to Los Angeles, I told my family I would be working for Stop AIDS Los Angeles, but not that the program was based at and funded by the Los Angeles Gay and Lesbian Center.

As we filed off the plane, Victoria remained upbeat. "You are such a special man," she said. "How could your parents possibly not continue to love and accept you?"

Her confidence did little to quell my jitters. I fell a few steps behind the women as we walked toward the baggage claim. I wasn't planning to come out until several days into my visit but still felt frightened. I asked myself, Do I look different? Have I assumed any mannerisms in L.A. that are going to give me away? I realized I already felt sad because I doubted coming out would happen the way I hoped. It was as if I were mourning a loss that hadn't yet occurred.

In the midst of mourning, I saw my father standing by the baggage carousel in his college professor drag—khaki pants, white short-sleeved shirt, blue striped tie; Tennessee weather in August precluded his polyester cardigan sweater. With his trim physique and thinning dirty blond hair, he was still a handsome, though fashion-challenged, man. I watched him for a few seconds, picturing him in a Brooks Brothers suit and an expensive haircut. As he said hello and stuck out his hand, I was jolted back to reality.

I introduced Dad to Victoria and Jane, then watched for his reaction, looking for signs of "guilt by association." Nothing. He politely shook their hands, then grabbed my bags and departed as I said good-bye to my friends.

As we headed for the car, I wanted my father to ask, "Are your friends lesbians?" Instead he said nothing. We walked through the parking lot in silence. I had been in Tennessee less than 15 minutes, hadn't even reached home, and my father and I had fallen into our familiar pattern. I would drop a hint about my life as a gay man, and he would ignore it.

I looked forward to not playing these games any longer but realized this would be no easy coming-out experience. My family had ignored a lot more obvious things than a quick introduction to a pair of lesbians. I had been working in the HIV education and prevention field for nearly two years and had not been involved with a woman during that time. But my parents still seemed clueless, able to ignore the blatantly obvious. The cornerstone of fundamentalist Christian faith sometimes seems to be "ignore it, and it will go away," a phenomenon I call "fundamental denial."

That is how they handled my job at Nashville Cares. After graduating from college, I briefly worked at a Huntsville, Ala., TV station, producing promotional spots for the news department. Friends and relatives, knowing I had left my news job and curious as to why, would confront my mother in their singsong Tennessee twang, "Toodie, what's that Stuart up to these days?"

My mother would answer with a half-truth, that I worked for the United Way, which partially funded Nashville Cares. "He's helping people," she would say if pressed. My parents did not mention publicly that many of the individuals I worked with were homosexuals, though in private they would commend me for charitably assisting "those people." But they were oblivious to the possibility that I or anyone else they loved might actually be one of those people.

The 30-minute car ride with my father to our home in Murfreesboro, a college town of 45,000, passed slowly. He and I had never been close and had experienced numerous run-ins. We were polar opposites. We disagreed on every political, social, and religious issue, but we shared the same intellectual capacity and strong verbal skills. Consequently, every conversation we had ended in a heated discussion, with each of us wanting to win at all costs. When I left Murfreesboro for Huntsville and then Nashville, we had tacitly established a verbal truce, a cease-fire that left us with little to say to each other. Now, trapped in the car, we alternated between silence and small talk that posed absolutely no danger of inciting an argument. I listened as he listed the latest family activities, and I answered his sterile queries about my apartment and the weather in California.

I wanted him to ask *real* questions about my life. For a moment I considered blurting out the truth, that his son is gay, a fag, a fairy. Instead, I watched the familiar roadside foliage roll past and remembered a bizarre rant nearly six years earlier.

My mother, my two younger sisters, and I were passing a rather droll Southern afternoon in the family kitchen, lunching on sandwiches and potato chips, discussing my return to college. After flunking out of the University of Tennessee, I had worked full time at a sporting-goods store for two years, set myself up in an apartment, and enrolled at the local college, Middle Tennessee State University. I had many fears about going back to school, though I felt more motivated and confident at 20 than I had at 18. We spoke of my class schedule, financial aid, and study habits. Suddenly, without warning, our afternoon was interrupted.

"You are garbage!" I turned to see that my father had entered the kitchen. He pointed a finger in my direction. "I am tired of finding trash like you in my house!"

My mother pleaded, "Alan, please stop," but he continued to yell. After several minutes I left, sobbing uncontrollably. My mother followed and tried to comfort me. I asked what I had done, and she had no answer, though she assured me she did not share my father's sentiments.

After that, I stopped by the house only when I knew my father wouldn't be there. But my mother, the emotional heart of the family, wanted my father and me to make peace. She got us to agree to a meeting in my father's study. Perhaps naively, I expected an apology. I was ready and willing to forgive and forget. But there was no apology, only a halfhearted, "Sorry if what I said hurt you." Frustrated, I asked why he would call me trash, telling him all I had ever wanted was his friendship.

"Well, Stuart," he said without looking at me, "if I weren't your father, you're not someone I would choose as a friend." His tone was as cold as his words. I was more hurt by the casual cruelty of his response than I had been by his name-calling the week before.

It's hard to believe now, but my father was once some-one whose company people enjoyed. Many family mem-bers have told me how much I resemble my father when he was younger, before he was "born again." He had many friends, and my parents socialized often. But in the early 1970s, when I was six or seven, he changed. Drastically. Suddenly he centered his life around his church and his faith. Once he was "saved," he withdrew from the world.

My brother, Monty, and I were presented with a new set of rules that restricted our access to anything "worldly." We couldn't go to a movie unless it was rated G. We couldn't bring home a record unless he had listened to it first. Our relatives began to view him as a stern figure. My aunts and uncles eventually reached the point where they no longer enjoyed his company; they didn't feel as if they could be themselves in his presence. I think they worried that if they said or did the wrong thing, he would correct them. My fa-ther's compassion was swallowed by his newfound Christ-ian fervor, his emotions turned off.

As we barreled down Interstate 24 toward Murfreesboro, I leaned against the hard headrest of my father's car and closed my eyes, wishing I had responded by asking him who, if not his child, he would choose as a friend, for he didn't really have any friends. He didn't spend time with anyone other than his immediate family, close relatives, and people in the church. He and the elders at the Believers' Chapel might describe themselves as friends, but theirs was an issue-oriented relationship, better characterized as acquaintanceship. Between his rejection of the secular world and his icy, intellectualized approach to his faith, my father had sealed himself off from the possibility of gregarious friendship. Seated next to him in the car, I saw him as a lonely person.

I never did discover the cause of his rage that afternoon, though I often wonder if his tirade might have been triggered by an innate sense of my blossoming struggle with homosexuality. I also sometimes wonder if my mother truly had no idea what caused his anger.

I lifted my head, opened my eyes, and refocused on the lush greenery. We were on the exit ramp of the interstate. A few minutes' drive brought us to the street where I had grown up, Dill Lane. As we neared the stone pillars that marked the entrance to our driveway, I felt relieved that the interminable ride was over. But I also felt a knot of anxiety in my stomach. Nothing would be the same after this visit.

My parents had bought our seven-acre farm in 1975 after falling in love with the rundown stone farmhouse. After it was remodeled, we left our suburban ranch-style home and moved to the farm, just outside the city limits. The grounds were in sorry disarray, and for years thereafter my brother and I spent our afternoons and weekends helping my father landscape. Our collective efforts paid off. In addition to a large vegetable garden, we also had grapevines and blackberry bushes—the latter a welcome feature since Mom makes the world's finest cobbler. In addition, my paternal grandfather supplied us with horses, which contributed to the gentlemen-farmer aspect of our life. Since there were no other children nearby, my brother and I welcomed the diversion of the horses. When I developed other interests in junior high school, though, I sold mine and put the proceeds toward an electric piano. Except for two eventful years in Indiana, my family has lived at the farm ever since.

My father turned into the long gravel driveway. The slightly bumpy ride woke the butterflies in my stomach, and I wished I'd flown directly back to California instead of stopping in Tennessee. On the left, on good-size lots, sat a couple of mobile homes. The people who lived there kept them up, but my mother always hated that the trailers were so close to our house. Decades-old refurbished elegance side by side with newfangled prefabs. Welcome to the rural South.

The noise of the car drew the family outside. My mother ran to me, arms outstretched. Right behind were my sisters, 17-year-old Amy and 12-year-old Abby. I opened the car door and was greeted by a trio of enormous smiles and engulfed in hugs and kisses.

My move to California marked the first time any of my parents' children had lived more than an hour away from home. Monty, the oldest, still resides less than a mile away with his wife, Barbara, and their five-year-old son, Justin.

They maintain daily contact with the family. This closeness is extremely important to my mother, as her joy in life revolves around her children and, more recently, around her grandson. This made my absence difficult for her.

Since my father brought born-again Christianity into the household, my mother had tried, in her own way, to lead the kind of life her husband wanted. But there was a crucial difference between the two. Aside from the hours he spent teaching marketing at the university, my father grew increasingly estranged from the secular world, while my mother was able to participate in both worlds. Her big-heartedness allowed her to be accepting of people who didn't agree with her religious beliefs, whereas my father brandished his religion as a sword. My mother had no need to hit people over the head with her beliefs. She just lived her life, representing her Christianity through loving actions, not harsh words.

For instance, her best friend had always been her sister, Brenda. Brenda had married my father's brother, Ray, and they lived only a few miles away. Brenda and Ray were Christians but led a typical middle-class American lifestyle. As such, they were a lot more liberal than my parents. They had even thrown a college graduation party for me, complete with an open bar. Mom and Dad refused to attend. For years I had enjoyed hanging out on summer afternoons by Aunt Brenda's pool, shooting the breeze and having a drink. As often as not, my mother would be there too. Although she didn't drink or approve of alcohol, she would lounge comfortably and share in our laughter over whatever silly things amused us that day. Her religious beliefs were strong, but not enough to ruin friendships.

My mother has had her share of disappointments, mostly with things that haven't happened according to her expectations. My father's family owned six department stores, and he was to inherit and run them. But he and his father had a falling-out. Dad quit the family business and returned to school. I imagine that when my mother married my father she expected she would soon be living a country-club lifestyle, that everything would be easy once her husband established himself in the family business. It didn't work out that way. The situation was compounded by the fact that my father refused to take money from his parents, sending back the checks they mailed him. My mother had to take care of two young boys *and* work to support her graduate-student husband—not what she had bargained for. But she never complained.

After putting my father through school, she was able to quit work for a few years. But by the time I was nine, she was eager to return. She found a job as a secretary at a grammar school, but immediately after she accepted it she discovered she was pregnant. So instead of keeping a job she wanted and enjoyed, Mom stayed home with my sister Amy. When Amy was ready to go to kindergarten, my mother found another job

in the school system, this time as secretary to the superinten-
dent. But she became pregnant again. She hasn't looked for
work since. Maybe she feels jinxed. Or maybe she gave up.

My mother seems resigned to her life. What joy she has
is derived from her children rather than herself. I have always felt that my father treated her in a cold, unloving way;
my brother and I used to wonder why she stayed married to
him. In my father's defense, however, I suspect he would
be far happier teaching at a Christian college, such as Oral
Roberts University in Oklahoma rather than at Tennessee
State. But Mother has made it clear that she wants to stay
close to her sister and the rest of her family, and he has ac-
quiesced to her desires on that one point.

I love my mother and am grateful for the role she played
as our family's emotional glue. As it turned out, though, her
ability to embrace worlds other than my father's was not as
great as I had thought.

A few years before moving to California, I had subtly
tried to inform my mother of my homosexuality. I had broken up with Margaret, my college girlfriend, and Mom
asked if I was "seeing any other girl." I responded testily,
telling her that not only was I not dating any women but
that she should never ask me a question about women
again. The more brazen my hints, though, the deeper she
moved into denial. Nevertheless, I persisted in believing
that on some level she knew—after all, we were close, and

mothers have a sixth sense about their children. The fact that she fretted over my "new lifestyle" seemed to confirm this, although since I had never flat out told her about being gay, she never mentioned exactly what she thought my irksome new lifestyle might entail. If pressed, she would only say, as she had in her letter, that she missed me and that she hated my being in California. Perhaps she hated my move to Los Angeles and my escape from the oppressive atmosphere of the Bible Belt. Perhaps she sensed it gave me a chance to understand, express, and revel in the emotions and sexual feelings that were so unacceptable in Tennessee.

We spent my first evening home catching up, my sisters competing for the spotlight to tell me about their latest boyfriends, tennis lessons, and school activities. Once, while Abby nattered on about some newsworthy event, I stole a glance at my mom. She was smiling, but her eyes were moist—moved by the mundane happiness of having her brood back in the nest. After the girls went to bed, she filled me in on family gossip, what little there was. I couldn't help but realize I would soon be providing new material.

My parents went to bed at 10 o'clock, as always. I said good night and climbed the spiral staircase to my childhood bedroom. So much in my life had changed since I had last lived here, but the room was the same as when Monty and I shared it as teenagers—a museum of American male adolescence circa 1978.

As I got ready for bed, I realized that neither my sisters nor my parents had asked about California or my new job. I was glad these subjects hadn't come up because, even though I had vowed to answer any questions honestly, no matter what, I wanted this first night back at home to be free of discord. I was aware everything might soon change and welcomed one last gentle memory of a home life I had always treasured.

After making the decision to come out to my parents, I had consulted two books on the subject, *Now That You Know* by Betty Fairchild and Nancy Hayward, and *Coming Out: A Gift of Love*, by Rob Eichberg. I also talked to coworkers at the Los Angeles Gay and Lesbian Center and to friends who had come out to their parents. Telling your family in person was highly recommended. If the news that you are gay comes as a shock, it's important for the parents to see you in the flesh, to see you are still the same son or daughter that you've always been. I agreed with this approach, so once I knew I would be attending the conference in Washington, I made plans to add on the trip home.

Fairchild and Hathaway, the mothers of a gay man and a lesbian, respectively, also recommended that you not tell your parents separately. Their reasoning is that if you are closer to one parent, that parent might try to dissuade you from telling the other, to "keep it our little secret." Even though one parent might take the news better than the other, it's important that the less-accepting parent not feel as if this news had been withheld, even if only for a short time.

A third piece of advice I planned to follow was to give my parents the information and then leave, thereby avoiding arguments caused more by shock than rational reflection. I planned to emphasize that I would be available to answer questions and provide additional information but that I wanted to give them time to process the news. To that end, I called one of my best friends, Donna, who still lived in Murfreesboro, and asked if she would pick me up right after I told my parents.

I planned to tell my brother and his wife on Thursday night, waiting until Saturday, after lunch, to tell my folks. Donna agreed to pick me up immediately afterward and take me to Nashville, where I would spend the remainder of the weekend with another friend. I would return to my parents' for dinner on Monday and then back to Nashville that evening to leave for Los Angeles the following morning.

Wednesday morning was sunny and cool; it looked as if we would have at least one day in Tennessee that wasn't unbearably humid. I lingered over coffee, watching Mother putter in the kitchen. She was eager to take me to Aunt Brenda's. The plan was to spend some time there, eat lunch out, and then shop.

I've always enjoyed shopping with my mother and Aunt Brenda. Most men I knew considered trips to the mall a form of torture. But I never minded the way my mother and aunt would linger over a table of marked-down linens. I was never bored. In fact, I would often join in, hunting for the right color or size or discussing whether a particular kitchen doodad was worth the price. Mom had to know that I was different. How could she not?

Much as I expected, the three of us had a great visit. Once we left the house, Mother and Aunt Brenda filled me in on every little change—which stores were new, who had been sick, whose daughter was engaged. Our last stop was Kmart, a fashionable place to shop in Murfreesboro.

The familiar big K sign and interior layout brought back one of my earliest memories. As a child, I was notorious for running around stores, looking at the merchandise, touching everything, fascinated by what was new and what was beautiful. I never seemed to be able to stay with my parents, and they constantly warned me that someday I would be lost forever. I must have been four or five when they decided to teach me a lesson. The whole family was in Kmart, where, predictably, I embarked on an exploration of the toy department. My parents allowed me to run off, then hid behind racks so that I couldn't see them. I searched and searched but couldn't find them. I got scared, terrified, and collapsed on the floor—a sobbing heap. My mother instantly materialized, scooped me up, and told me they had been there all the time and that in the future I should listen and stay with her.

I never wandered off again. But I had nightmares for the remainder of my childhood in which my parents were killed in a car wreck and I was left all alone. I would fall back to sleep wondering what it would be like to be an orphan, the lonely child of deceased parents. It struck me as a terrible fate. The only thing that I could imagine being worse was to know that my family was alive but didn't want me.

As I prepared to come out to my family, I hoped my childhood nightmares were irrational fears, that my loving and supportive family would accept me—if not right away, then eventually. An overlying theme of *Now That You Know* is that even though some parents initially have difficulty with the news that their child is gay, they all come around. Nevertheless, I expected that my fundamentalist-Christian-enhanced coming-out experience would be a little rougher than most. So I fretted endlessly over how to best handle the events on Saturday, rehearsing speeches, anticipating questions, dreaming futile dreams of hugs all around.

After shopping I called some college friends to confirm plans for that night. Mother, meanwhile, pulled out all the new pictures of my nephew. We sat in the living room, and she passed me photos, one after another, a pictorial history of almost every step Justin had taken in the six months I had been away.

Mom kept separate albums for each of her four children, documenting our progress from infancy to adulthood. She cherished the albums almost as much as she cherished the kids.

"Are you planning on making a photo album for Justin?" I asked.

"I think so," Mother replied. "I hope it's OK with Monty and Barbara."

I doubted they would mind and told her so.

"Do you think I could have my album?" I asked. "You know, take it back to California?"

She shook her head and told me that she couldn't part with it.

"It's just that I have no pictures of my childhood out there, and I miss you all."

"Monty wants his album too," she said. "But I really can't give them up."

I reached out and squeezed her hand. I just knew that this woman had so much love for her children that she wouldn't have any problem with my news.

That evening, like every evening, we ate dinner at 6 o'clock. The Miller household runs on a schedule: laundry on Monday and Thursday, chores before breakfast and immediately after school, dinner at 6, bedtime at 10, and so on. Until I went to college, I thought that was the norm. I am still occasionally surprised by the lack of regimentation at friends' houses, where people sit in different spots from one meal to the next.

When I was a kid, dinner took 15 or 20 minutes. My father's ability to turn any conversation into a sermon taught Monty and me to keep our table talk limited and as generic as possible. We were rarely able to engage in a conversation about anything other than the Bible. Other topics were worldly and therefore not worthy of our Christian attention. And after every dinner we stayed at the table for family Bible study.

During college, and later when I was living in Nashville, I would come home every few weeks. Often these visits weren't planned—no need to call in advance since the family rarely ate out, and there was always enough food for one more. I would just show up at 6 o'clock, earlier if I wanted to do my wash. Homework was a convenient excuse to leave before Bible study, though my father frowned on that practice.

On this trip I wanted to enjoy the time with my family, and that enjoyment didn't include immersion in fundamentalist dogma. So at 6:20, I stood, thanked Mother for a lovely meal, and announced that I was going out to visit with friends. My father, as he had done so many times over the years when I skipped out on Bible talk to "study," pursed his lips but said nothing.

The next day passed in another round of errands and family visits. I was grateful for the distractions, since I planned to speak to Monty that evening. Menial tasks kept me somewhat relaxed. I practiced my coming-out speech and worried more about the main event with my parents than this preliminary round with my brother.

And then it was time.

Monty is three years older than I am. Barbara, is my age. In fact, she was one of my closest childhood friends. We were raised in the same church—an interesting choice of words fundamentalist Christians use, "raised in the church"—where our fathers were both elders. As a result, there was a powerful bond between Barbara and me, one that perhaps only those brought up in similar circumstances can understand.

Monty and Barbara eloped to get married, which caused a tremendous stir in both families and throughout the congregation. My brother and Barbara learned early, as I had, that when dealing with fundamentalists it is often easier to be manipulative and deceitful than honest and forthright—even in such serious matters as marriage. The passage of time, the birth of a grandchild, and Monty and Barbara's happiness had healed any visible wounds, and their marriage was now considered a success.

My brother and I have always differed. Like the Donny and Marie anthem we used to sing so fervently, he is a little bit country, and I'm a little bit rock and roll. When I was at college having the time of my life, he was starting a business.

When I was questioning my sexuality, he was raising a child. He is happiest with horses, cars, tractors, and farming. I'm more interested in music, theater, and intellectual pursuits. But despite our many differences, he had always been there for me. In the time-honored tradition of older brothers, Monty believed it was fine if he picked on me, but he made certain no one else did. Given that Monty and Barbara had once "broken the rules" themselves, I suspected they would react rationally to the news they were about to hear.

When I arrived, Monty and Barbara had just finished dinner and were getting their three-foot-tall tornado of a son off to bed. We sat in the den, *Wheel of Fortune* on television, and discussed the family. Monty had a poor relationship with our father, too, so whenever we got together, that's what we talked about. Now that we were no longer kids sharing a room, the fact that neither of us got along with Dad was the glue that bound us together.

Having heard our gripes before, Barbara tuned us out and concentrated on the show, punctuating Monty's and my talk with staccato outbursts:"*t*" or "buy an *a*."

I waited until the final spin had revealed that night's winner before saying that I needed to tell them something important. They both tensed, bracing for bad news. Monty, forever and always controller of the remote, clicked off the TV.

I took a deep breath. "There's something I've known about myself for a long time, and I wanted to share it with you." I poured out my story, telling them I am gay and had always known it, even though it had taken me many years and a great deal of courage to accept the fact. They listened quietly. I let them know I was happy and then waited for their reaction.

Barbara spoke first. "Are you sure?" Tears streamed down the soft lines of her face.

"I've always known. I've known since I was a little kid."

I looked at Monty and asked, "Didn't you already suspect?"

He nodded, indicating he did.

I let myself relax for a moment.

Barbara, a nurse, asked about my health.

"You don't have to worry. I'm HIV-negative."

Soon enough—inevitably, invariably—we returned to the topic of our parents. I told Monty and Barbara that I had planned my entire trip in order to tell Mom and Dad I was gay.

"What's the point?" Monty asked. "They won't understand."

Barbara seconded his opinion. "They're not going to accept it. Ever. Why tell them? You live 3,000 miles away—it doesn't matter."

"I can't live with the dishonesty," I said. "Someday I want to share my life with someone, the way the two of you have. Why should it be that just because I'm gay I could never bring that person home?"

Monty and Barbara understood my wish to settle down with someone special. My sister-in-law said, "Well, you're right. If you care about somebody and you love someone, you should have the same rights we have."

My brother volunteered to be with me when I told Mom and Dad.

I was touched by the offer. "Thank you," I said. "But it's better if I do this on my own. There's no point in your getting involved. Plus, you'll need to stay out of it now, because I may need your support later. Mom and Dad should think you're objective." I paused, then asked, "Do they have a gun in the house?"

Monty and I had been raised hearing our father make statements like, "In Biblical times disobedient children were stoned by their families." He had never been violent, but I still remembered a time in Indiana when he threatened to "put me in the emergency room." I didn't want him to snap.

My brother assured me that my parents kept no guns.

When it was time to leave, Monty and Barbara walked me to the door. My typically stoic brother surprised me with a hug. "I love you," he said. His gesture, one I'll always remember, was as unexpected as it was gallant.

Friday passed in another round of family visits and errands. Despite the relative ease of the encounter with my brother and sister-in-law, I was a wreck, though no one seemed to notice. I obsessed over every possible outcome of the impending conversation with my parents. I knew from past experience that I wasn't being too pessimistic to expect the worst.

I had always been a good kid but by no means perfect. I never shared my parents' rigid sensibilities. As a result, I often lied to them, the lies increasing in frequency and scope as I grew older.

Just before my sophomore year of high school, my father took a position at Ball State University. Except for Monty, who had graduated from high school and taken a job in Murfreesboro, we moved to Muncie, Ind., which seemed amazingly metropolitan after so many years in small-town Tennessee. At my new school I worked hard to fit in with the "right" crowd. But my parents worried, convinced I spent too much time with the wrong sort of people. My friends were honor students, athletes, and student government leaders, but Mom and Dad feared these secular teens would sway me from my fundamentalist Christian mores.

I suppose they did, too, to a certain extent. I experimented with alcohol and began smoking cigarettes, facts I kept hidden from my parents. Still, my friends and I were wholesome Midwestern teenagers. We tested our limits, as adolescents do. But we were never discipline problems. We were absolutely *not* bad kids.

Near the end of my junior year, the parents of one of my friends were out of town and, not surprisingly, we planned an all-night party. Since I was not allowed to stay out late or spend the night with friends, I knew I would have to leave the party at just about the time everyone else arrived. Tired of missing out, I developed an elaborate scheme to circumvent my curfew. The ruse included an appeal to my father's religious fervor—a stroke of genius that was also my downfall.

I typed a letter on the stationery of my girlfriend's church, inviting me to attend a nonexistent weekend "youth retreat" as the guest of her family and parish. I devised an elaborate schedule—everything from nature walks and making s'mores to discussions on interpreting the Bible—all to convince my overly protective parents that the retreat was just what their wayward son needed.

My parents agreed not only that I could go but also that I should go, even though my father would be away at an academic conference and Mother would be left alone.

My father left town, and I triumphantly went to my "retreat." My mother, however, unearthed the truth. She telephoned the party and ordered me home. Trapped in a web of my own weaving, I obeyed. She and I stayed up late, fighting, crying, and discussing what to do. I apologized over and over and begged her not to tell my father, to let me tell him instead. She eventually agreed.

As it turned out, though, her promise was only as good as my forgery. On Monday, when I arrived home from school, my parents were waiting for me in the living room. My father motioned for me to take a seat. I did, noticing he held a Bible. "You are a Jacob," he began, his voice controlled but angry. "Jacob means liar. In Biblical times disobedient children and liars were stoned by their parents." I had heard this before but never with such vehemence.

He continued for 30 minutes. I remained in my chair, silent, not allowed to speak. He told me I should thank my mother for having told him of my deceit when I was not home. "Otherwise," he said, "you'd be in the emergency room instead of the living room." He grounded me until I turned 18 and ordered me to quit all my school activities. He told me that my girlfriend's parents would be notified of our plan to "spend the night in sin."

Although I might have preferred a stoning, I did not consider this punishment inordinate. I knew what I had done was wrong. But being grounded for more than six months was not the end of my father's sentence. He contacted the vice principal of my high school. I worked for her as an office aide during my free period and considered her a friend and confidante. His letter to her said I was a liar who could not be trusted.

And then he delivered the crowning blow.

Without warning, he quit his job and moved our family back to Tennessee, eventually finding a job teaching at Tennessee State University. His hope, I am sure, was that once I was home again, I would regain my Christian sensibility and reject my rebellious ways.

As I lay in bed recalling this confrontation with my father, I became more and more frightened about my parents' possible reaction to my announcement. Would they tell me they already knew and that it didn't matter because they loved me anyway? Would they throw me out and tell me to never come home again? Would Dad resort to the physical violence he had threatened in Indiana? I tormented myself until I drifted off to sleep.

After breakfast on Saturday morning, I wrote a short note to my aunt and uncle. I knew I wasn't going to have a chance to come out to them in person. I didn't want to tell them before my parents and wouldn't have time afterward. But I did want them to know. I wanted to make sure my parents, especially my mother, would not isolate themselves with my news. I thought it might make things easier if I told Brenda and Ray. And I was confident that my aunt and uncle would support me as they had so many times before. They would help my parents accept things, even if they were uncomfortable with my news.

As I packed my bags, I reviewed my plan one last time. Tell them you have something important to share. Say you are gay, that you have always been gay, but that you have denied it for many years. Let them know they did nothing to "make this happen." Tell them that you love them. And throughout, show them you are the same Stuart they raised and have known for 26 years. Show them the book you want them to read and explain that when you return on Monday, you will be willing to talk some more.

The time had come. D-day.

I carried my bags downstairs and placed them by the door, ready for a quick escape. Then, *Now That You Know* in one hand, my speech in the other, I asked my parents to join me in the living room. "There's something I want to tell you," I said.

I braced for a confrontation, just as I had at age 17 in Indiana. Except this time I would be the one talking. My mother probably imagined I was going to tell them I had AIDS since she harbored irrational fears about my working with HIV-positive people. She sat in her favorite chair, ashen. My father took a seat at one end of our lengthy couch, as near as he could be to his wife without actually sharing her blue chair. I sat at the other end, miles away. They waited for me to begin.

It was 1 o'clock. Donna would arrive at 1:30. Thirty minutes to change our lives.

I had rehearsed my speech endlessly, but my mind was blank. I grinned nervously, took a deep breath, and peeked at my notes.

"Mom, Dad," I finally began, "there is no easy way for me to tell you this, so I'm just going to say it. I'm gay. I've known it for a long time and I wanted you to know."

I told them I loved them, then gave them my copy of *Now That You Know*. "This book was written by two mothers with gay children. I've read it. I'd like you to have it. I know this probably isn't easy, and I'm willing to answer any questions you might have."

My mother stared out the window at the front yard, examining everything but me.

My father said, "I want you to know that we're glad you told us this." He was calm. He didn't even raise his voice. "God is going to take care of this."

Maybe this is going to be OK, I thought.

"The first thing we need to do is to acknowledge the fact that you're homosexual," he said. "And then we can begin the process of change." He launched into a litany of how "we" were going to "fix" things. He lectured as if this were a lesson he had prepared for his classroom to take his students from point A to point B.

It was good for him and Mother to know, he said, because only through that knowledge could they help me overcome my "lifestyle choice." They would pray to save me. "We're going to read the Bible together. The Bible says…"

I interrupted. "Wait a minute. I don't think you understand. I don't want to change. I'm happy the way I am. That you believe this is a choice that can be changed isn't relevant. This is who I am. I'm not asking for help, only acceptance. I wanted to give you an important piece of information about my life."

"You know what the Bible says about this, don't you? Do you believe in the Bible?" He started quoting Scripture, proselytizing on the "clear" words the Bible spoke about the "abomination" of homosexuality. As a child of God, he would not and could not tolerate its existence, he said.

My mother sat in silence, still staring out the window.

I reiterated that this was the way I was created and that I shared my secret with them out of honesty and love, not a desire to change.

My protests were ignored. Dad forged ahead as if he hadn't heard me. He believed we could "solve this problem" if we all worked together.

After about ten minutes, his lesson came to an abrupt end. "That's all I have to say for now." He turned to my mother.

"Toodie, do you have anything that you want to add?"

"He knows how I feel," Mother said.

I had never heard her speak in such an icy tone. My father's dispassionate, professorial reaction was not surprising. But I had expected an emotional response from Mother—crying, screaming, a sympathetic statement that she loved me and had always known—but not this.

Before anyone could say more, the phone rang. Donna on her car phone. "Should I come up now?" she asked, "or give you more time?"

I told her I would be right out.

I grabbed my bags and asked, "Is it OK if I come back Monday for dinner?"

"Of course," said my father. "Of course, it's OK."

"Well, I'll see y'all at 6 then. We can talk more then if you like."

At the back door my mother said "good-bye." That was it, nothing more. She didn't hug me. She didn't even look at me.

"Be careful this weekend," my father said. Maybe he was operating on autopilot. He hadn't said anything like that to me since I was a teenager.

I fell into Donna's car. She took my hand, then pulled away from the house. She didn't attempt a conversation, for which I was grateful. I slipped the letter to Aunt Brenda and Uncle Ray into their mailbox on our way out of town, and we headed for Nashville.

It was over. I had done what I set out to do.

Donna pulled over and handed me some tissues. I hadn't realized until then that I was crying. "It's going to be OK," she said.

Through my tears, I explained what had happened. Donna told me to be patient. "Time heals," she said. I hoped she was right, that my parents would come around. But I knew that fundamentalist Christianity is a life that knows no gray, only black and white, right and wrong, good and evil. It was conceivable that my parents would never accept or love a gay son.

By the time we arrived in Nashville at my friend Phil's house, I had stopped crying.

"Do you want me to go in with you?" Donna asked. Phil was going to be out all afternoon but had told me where a set of keys was hidden. "We could have some iced tea."

"Thanks. But if you don't mind, I need to be by myself."

I dropped my bags inside the front door and stumbled to the guest room. I wanted to sleep. Some people can't sleep when they're upset. They replay the scene over and over or imagine eight different versions of what might happen next. But I'm not like that. When I'm depressed or upset, I sleep.

I collapsed on the bed and was out in seconds.

Four hours later, I woke to the sound of music playing softly in the back of the house. I sat, rubbed my eyes, shook off my postnap grogginess, and said "hello" to Phil, who was in the den reading.

I had met Phil through Nashville Cares and hadn't seen him for months. At dinner I tried to keep as much of the conversation on him as I could, telling him how things had gone, but saying I didn't want to think or talk about it. Phil was not out to his family, and I didn't want to scare him by focusing on my parents' less-than-enthusiastic reaction.

After dinner we met up with a group of friends, and I proceeded to drink my way to numb oblivion. Even surrounded by friends, I felt desperately alone. I couldn't get into the party spirit. I felt as if I had a bad head cold and was full of medication. I was functioning but in a fog. Still, it seemed better to be out with friends than sitting alone worrying about what had happened and what might happen next.

The next morning I felt as if my brain had been sucked through a tiny hole drilled into the base of my skull. My new life of truthfulness was off to an agonizingly painful start. I pulled myself together as best I could and telephoned John, a friend and coworker from Nashville Cares who lived down the street from Phil. He was home and suggested I join him for coffee.

I planned on a light social visit. I would be the old buddy back in town, talking up the good life, L.A.-style. But John is a social worker—a good one—adept at ferreting out and addressing emotional issues. A few well-directed questions, and I was crying, spilling my guts.

"It sounds like you're punishing yourself over this," John said, "which you shouldn't be doing. Why should you feel shame about coming out?"

I shrugged.

"Did you tell them this to hurt them?"

"Of course not."

"Then stop punishing yourself. Their response wasn't what you wanted, but that doesn't cancel the fact that you did this out of love. You should be telling yourself, 'I did the right thing.' And you're going to have to move on regardless of your parents' reaction."

It was comforting and enlightening to spend the afternoon with someone as perceptive as John. He was fair and evenhanded toward my parents, engaging me in a discussion about what it must be like for parents to learn their child is gay. "Step back from what you're in right now, and look at it from their standpoint," he said. "At the same time, remember that you haven't done anything wrong. You didn't set out to hurt them."

He reminded me that many gay men and lesbians worry that disclosure of their sexuality will disappoint their parents, as if coming out were an admission of second-class citizenship. I had developed and led workshops centered around similar concerns for gay men dealing with HIV, and John suggested I start listening to my own advice. He also stressed that I needed to work through my own issues, even as I gave my parents time to work through theirs.

I left John's feeling hopeful and more at peace than I had in weeks. Coming out is an enormous strain, and I had handled myself OK. I would be able to go back home the next night for dinner with the family.

On Monday morning I telephoned my friend Scott. We would be driving to California the next day with all of his belongings. An actor, he had decided it was time to seek his fortune in Hollywood. Even better, he planned to stay with my roommate and me until he found his own place.

In the meantime he let me borrow his car for the quick trip to Murfreesboro. I headed toward home, relatively calm, but mentally prepared for a big confrontation, or at the very least an emotional discussion. I anticipated questions: How do you know you're gay? Have you had sex with men? Have you tried to change?

A place was set for me at the table. "Hi," I said.

My father motioned for me to take a chair. I sat, and he immediately bowed his head in prayer. As we began to eat, I realized that Mother and Father had not told my sisters and that they had no intention of doing so over dinner. Mom steered the conversation toward small talk, still unable to look at me, and my unsuspecting sisters carried the conversation.

Twenty minutes later, my father stood and invited me to watch a football game on TV with him. It was one of the first games of the new season, he said, and he didn't want to miss it. "No, thanks," I answered. "I think I'll stay in here and talk to Mom." The girls scurried away, and Mom and I were alone.

"Well," I said. "What's going on?"

She had been rinsing the dishes but stopped abruptly. "You know, I think I'm going to watch the ball game with your dad, so I guess you had better just go on."

I couldn't believe it. They knew this would be our last chance to talk before I returned to California. But I decided to follow their lead. You've dropped an enormous surprise on them, I thought. Don't force it. If they don't want to talk right now, don't make them. By the time you're back for Thanksgiving, they'll have had three months to digest this.

When my father heard me leaving, he stood and shook my hand. "Don't be a stranger. You know you're always welcome here."

I thanked my father just as cordially, and then I headed toward the door. Mom followed me out, her hands behind her back. When I reached Scott's car, I turned and said, "I'm sorry if I've hurt you. That wasn't what I meant to do."

For the first time since I had told them I am gay, she looked me in the eye. "I have always supported and taken up for you," she said, "and now you've stabbed me in the back."

"Mom, this was about my telling you something. Something important in my life. Not about stabbing you in the back or—"

She interrupted. "How could you do this to me?"

"Please don't take this personally. You haven't done anything," I said.

"Obviously I have," she replied. "Obviously I've been a terrible mother because if I had raised you the right way, the way God intended, you wouldn't be this way."

This was going all wrong.

"Things will never be the same," she said, hands still behind her back. "Part of me died on Saturday."

"Why don't you read the book I gave you?" I asked. "And by the time I'm home at Thanksgiving, we'll be able to talk about this rationally."

"I don't think Thanksgiving's a good idea," she answered. "I'm not sure you're welcome in your aunt's house."

I felt as if I had been slapped across the face. I knew this would be difficult, but I never once thought my family would actually shut me out.

Before I could recover, she followed up with another blow, the first bomb in what I now call "the prayer war."

"I want you to have this," she announced as her arms came into view at last. She was holding my photo album, the same one she hadn't been able to part with a few days earlier.

"Well…thanks," I managed to say.

I repeated that I loved her. She echoed my sentiment, but her words were cold and flat.

She turned away as I climbed into the car. I kept hoping she would look back, but she walked to the house and disappeared inside.

As I turned the ignition and started down the driveway, I suddenly realized my worst childhood nightmare had come true. My parents were alive and well, but they no longer wanted me as their son.

CHAPTER 2

TACTICAL RETREAT

I was numb the next morning as I drove to pick up Scott. After dating seriously and breaking up disastrously, Scott and I had become close friends. He had recently decided to move to Los Angeles to join my roommate, John, and me as the third tenant in our West Hollywood apartment. He had never made a cross-country trip, and I had agreed to accompany him.

I pulled into his family's driveway to find him waiting with his things, a human buoy floating in a sea of boxes and suitcases. He flashed his perfect smile, the one that still made me melt, and I wondered how he expected to cram a lifetime's accumulation into his tiny car. I popped the trunk, and we began loading.

"So how was the Last Supper?'" he asked as we worked, sensing my dour mood and aware that religious sarcasm nearly always helps to cheer me up. He flashed that great smile again.

I tried to return his grin but couldn't.

"Are you OK?" he asked. He patted me on the shoulder; the much-needed hug would have to wait until we were away from his parents. Even though they knew he was gay, they never discussed it. An overt display of affection was out of the question. So we finished packing, said our good-byes, and drove off.

My first love. We had met nearly two years earlier, in Nashville, through the AIDS agency I worked for. He had sent a letter of complaint about the lack of flexibility in our volunteer training schedule. I telephoned, apologized, and assured him I would do everything in my power to make any future experience he had with our agency more positive.

The following weekend we met accidentally at a local bar, and I instantly fell in love, or at least into a fantasy of the two of us riding giant palomino horses down a deserted stretch of Caribbean beach. An actor with New York soap opera and television guest star roles to his credit, he was different from the other men in Nashville. He maintained his down-home charm but knew about life in the big city. I fell fast and hard and spent the duration of our relationship in ecstasy, little realizing first loves almost never work out.

As we neared Highway 40, Scott pulled over and took a good look at his silently weeping passenger. Comprehending the magnitude of the situation, he seethed with the anger I was still too numb to feel. After hugging me he turned and unfurled his lanky middle finger in the direction of Murfreesboro. Then we sped off. I am certain he would have "burned rubber" had we been in a slightly more potent vehicle.

We traveled without speaking, immersed in the pounding beat of techno, until we passed the WELCOME TO ARKANSAS, BILL CLINTON GOVERNOR sign. Scott's rage over my parents' treatment of me had subsided, or maybe he had tired of my pouting and the loud music. He pointed at my lap, to the photo album I clutched. "Aren't you going to look at that?" he asked.

I had been holding the book tightly enough and long enough to leave permanent fingertip imprints but was surprised to find it in my hands. "No. I'm not." And then I lifted the plastic-encased cover and journeyed back to the childhood—the life—I had just left behind.

I leafed through the pages. Me as a baby. My brother and me dressed in authentic Japanese outfits my grandparents had bought on a trip to the Orient, his skinny little-boy arm draped over my pudgy toddler shoulders. My father, mother, brother, and I displaying our beachwear on a stretch of Florida sand. The four of us again, this time in front of the small home we lived in while Dad attended graduate school. A picture of my brother, my mother, and me with my paternal grandparents. An identical picture with my maternal grandparents.

I searched for a picture of the two sets of grandparents together but did not find one. Odd, since both Miller sons had married Howell daughters and the two couples lived only 15 miles apart.

My paternal grandparents, the Millers, were "city" folks—refined, with old money and power. Grandfather Miller had been mayor of his town and owned a string of department stores. My father was raised with the privileges of wealth—status, private schools, vacations—though he seemed to resent his family, especially his father.

My maternal grandparents, the Howell's, on the other hand, were "country" folks. My mother grew up with neither money nor social standing. Nanny Howell had told us many times the story of how when she and Granddaddy Howell first married, she had only one dress and had to wash it every day. Years of hard work and sweaty toil paid off, though, and now the Howells owned a successful dairy farm and lived in a large, beautiful farmhouse furnished with expensive antiques. The only thing that appealed more to Nanny Howell than antiques were diamonds. Earrings, pendants, necklaces, rings, bracelets—if it came with a diamond, she owned it.

My first seven summers were spent with my mother and brother visiting first the Howells and then the Millers.

Mother would herd her babies into the family car each June and drive north, leaving my father behind in Auburn, and later in Fayetteville, to work on his graduate degrees. My brother and I loved each set of grandparents dearly. We cherished our visits to the Howell's country farm where we milked cows and rode horses, as well as our visits to the Miller's city house where we sipped iced tea and gorged ourselves on Mayfield's Brown Cow Ice Cream Bars. I'm sure my brother preferred the farm, but my best memories are of times spent in the city with Nanny Miller. I loved her laugh, her glamour, and her excessive willingness to indulge me.

In the car with Scott, I flipped forward through the album to a favorite picture of me, age three, wearing a straw hat and a coquettish grin. Even at a young age I knew how to strike a pose. I smiled for the first time in what seemed like an eternity. "Did I ever tell you about my purse?"

Scott laughed. "No. I missed that one."

"Nanny Miller gave me a purse when I was four years old," I told him. Evidently taken by the flashiness of hers, I constantly demanded to be the bearer of her bag. She had tired of me breaking up her expensive matching "outfits" and eventually gave me an older purse she no longer carried. Medium-sized and made of black textured cloth with a faux wooden clasp running its entire length, the purse was filled with tissues, hand lotion, and a set of fake diamond ear bobs. I was in heaven. The bag became my most treasured possession, much to the chagrin of my father. I insisted on carrying it at all times, though I knew, even as a small boy, this was unacceptable behavior.

The next winter, after spending the holidays with family in Tennessee, we drove back to Auburn on a cold, rainy night. Along the way we stopped for dinner at Krystals, a fast-food restaurant indigenous to the South that serves tiny square hamburgers steeped in grilled onions—my favorite fast food to this day. Before leaving the restaurant, my mother suggested I go to the rest room since it might be my last chance, a polite way of reminding me that my father didn't like to stop when he drove, especially not for something as tedious as one of his children needing to urinate. I grabbed my purse and scampered to the men's room. After "doing my business" I applied a dab of Nanny Miller's hand cream, admired myself in the mirror modeling my ear bobs, and then beat a hasty retreat to rendezvous with my family at the car.

As we drove off I recoiled in horror. I had left my purse in the rest room. My beautiful purse! No amount of crying or pleading could persuade my father to turn the car around, and I received no replacement purse from my grandmother—at my father's request, no doubt. He may not have been in Tennessee to halt the gift of the first purse, but even as a relatively young man he had a way of making himself clearly understood. His loving mother would not make the same mistake twice.

Scott laughed at my story. "I guess that explains your choice of Halloween costumes," he said, pointing to a photo of my brother and me. Monty is dressed as a cowboy. I'm dressed as my mother.

Scott and I both laughed hysterically.

After my father finished his master's degree, we moved from Auburn, Ala., to Fayetteville, Ark., where he began his doctoral studies in marketing, and I started grammar school. I began to realize I was different from the other little boys, though you would never know it by looking at my first-grade class photo. I'm a gap-toothed, smiling face in the back row wearing a hideous orange-and red-striped polyester shirt. At school I enjoyed "girl" games more than "boy" games; my classmates called me sissy to reinforce this knowledge. At home, my brother played sports outside with the neighborhood boys while I stayed indoors playing private fantasy games.

One spring afternoon, as my brother played baseball in the backyard with friends, I locked myself in my room and daydreamed of becoming a glamorous Hollywood starlet. Carried away, I took off my clothes and tucked my penis between my legs to look like one of the women in the magazines my father kept hidden in the bottom drawer of his bedside table. The magazines disappeared after he was "born again." I lolled on my bed, nude, posing, sublime, until I was jolted back to reality by childish laughter and singsong chants of "Stuart wants to be a girl! Stuart wants to be a girl!" My brother and his friends had abandoned their baseball game and chosen this inopportune moment to spy on me through my bedroom window.

I did not share this story with Scott and closed my scrapbook almost as quickly as my flushed, naked, six-year-old arms had whipped my bedroom curtains shut so many years before. At that singular childhood moment, I realized being different was not acceptable. After that I worked hard to be more masculine and fit in.

In the car I ate some crackers, opened the last of our six-pack of Coke, and decided to watch the nation roll past. But a few miles of the dull Oklahoma landscape sent me back to my photo album. As depressing as the pictures might have been, they were at least in color.

I opened to a photo of me on Easter Sunday in Fayetteville. "I remember this picture," I said to Scott. "This was right after we converted to Southern Baptist." My first Easter without the Easter Bunny, the year my father decided the Easter Bunny and Santa Claus were pagan symbols unsuitable for his "born again" family.

"I thought your church was nondenominational," said Scott.

"It is," I answered. "But before that we were Southern Baptist, and before that…"

The first six years of my life we were Methodists and not devout. We went to church on Sunday morning but rarely discussed God or religion. To me, church meant I had to bathe, dress in my good clothes, and sit quietly for an hour. Sometimes my mother would give me a stick of chewing gum, Wrigley's spearmint, or a pen and some paper to play with. Neither my brother nor I were expected to listen, though we did sing the hymns.

And then it changed.

While my mother, brother, and I were visiting my grandparents, my father took a break from his studies to attend a religious revival, an "expo." Expos were all the rage in the early '70s Bible Belt as college-educated 20-somethings searched desperately for meaning in their lives. *Born again* and *saved* became buzzwords for young conservatives across the South. My father was not immune to the allure.

We returned to Fayetteville at the end of the summer and were greeted by a man much different than the one we had left behind. Although still the same height and weight, with the same haircut, glasses, and clothes, my father had changed—subtly, but enough that even I could see it.

This familiar but strange man told his family he had been reborn, that once he had been an empty vessel but now was full, inhabited by Christ. I was confused, as were my brother and mother. My father repeated himself several times and invited us to kneel and join him in the salvation prayer.

"Alan," my mother said, "I'm not sure about this." But my father was not a man to be denied—a trait too ingrained to disappear, even in rebirth. We kneeled and began to pray with him.

The following Sunday we attended an evangelical Southern Baptist Church instead of our traditional Methodist service. My mother protested, but, as always, my father's word was law.

Our new church stood as a perfect example of evangelical fundamentalism. A huge choir belted out passionate hymns. The pastor raged about the need for salvation and a personal relationship with Jesus. The services were infinitely more entertaining than those at the sedate Methodist church we had been attending, but I was distressed to discover that gum and doodling were no longer permitted.

Within weeks I walked to the altar and invited Christ to live in my heart and save me from eternal damnation. I felt no different after being "saved" but was happy I had made my father so proud. Mother said she had already invited Jesus into her life and held out as long as she could. But eventually she also "recommitted" herself to Jesus.

At home, we prayed before meals, something we had previously done only on rare occasions. Afterward, my father would read from the Bible, quizzing his wife and young sons on the meaning of whatever passage he had just read.

After my father finished graduate school and a one-year stint at Marshall University in Huntington, W.V., we moved back to Tennessee. Mother was thrilled. My father had secured a job as an associate professor of marketing at Middle Tennessee State University, and we would be living in the same town as Brenda and Ray. My mother and Brenda grew closer than ever. My father, on the other hand, alienated a large portion of both sides of the family through his incessant preaching. As he stepped closer to God, he distanced himself from anyone, family and friends included, who did not share his fundamentalist views.

At family gatherings my father would say grace. Prayers that had once been a step past "Rub-a-dub-dub, thanks for the grub" became his personal forums, golden opportunities to convert the wayward to the teachings of the Lord. As he proselytized endlessly, I would sit and watch his audience. Eyebrows would raise, eyes would roll and eventually glaze over. My mother's attempts to make excuses for his behavior were painful to watch.

My father's impromptu sermons lasted every bit as long as those at our new church but were not nearly as entertaining. Our elderly hellfire-and-brimstone-preaching pastor's favorite Bible story was the one about Jezebel where the Godly men rant "Fling her down! Fling her down!" and he put on a show every time he told it. His favorite phrase was "Ain't God good?"

The man oozed old-fashioned evangelism but suffered from an unfortunate lack of schooling. The arrival of a recently recruited associate pastor—young, personable, well-educated—spelled trouble for the aging minister. Grace Baptist's congregation split, older churchgoers loyal to their longtime shepherd, younger members following their new recruit. The unity of our tiny church wilted, then burned. From the ashes sprang forth a new church—Believers' Chapel—led by the younger pastor.

Founded by my father and three other men, Believers' Chapel does not belong to any denomination. Instead, it holds to the "true" teachings of the Bible.

"Your father founded the church?" asked Scott. "You never told me that."

"Yes," I said, "like Jim Jones without the Kool Aid."

For several years my life blended easily with our religion, and I was happy as a member of Believers' Chapel. Overweight and effeminate, I possessed little chance of running with the "in" crowd, so I spent my time practicing the piano, doing chores, and wishing I could be skinny and popular. I also began performing in church, playing piano under the supervision of the pastor's wife, Mary Lee. She would sing tearful solos to my accompaniment, my pudgy fingers ringing almost as true as her magnificent voice. These performances were the highlight of my life and provided a sense of belonging that I otherwise lacked.

I turned pages in my scrapbook to a shot of me at the piano, pudgy and smiling, Mary Lee behind me with bright red big-Texas hair and heavy makeup, looking like a relative of Tammy Faye Bakker.

About the time the picture with Mary Lee was taken, I began experiencing what I knew were "wicked" dreams, usually involving older boys or men. I would wake from these dreams, sweaty and scared, to find a disturbingly sticky wetness in my underwear. I hadn't had the facts of life explained to me and believed the nighttime mess was punishment from God for my evil dreaming. Every Sunday I prayed for redemption so that I would stop having those awful dreams. But my prayers went unanswered.

I remained ignorant about the changes in my body until my brother, in high school at the time, brought home a *Penthouse* magazine. Our parents were away for the evening, and he had a date, so he told me I could look at it as long as I didn't "mess it up," leaving me to wonder just exactly how he supposed I might mess it up.

The pictures were similar to the photos I had seen in my father's magazines so many years before, though infinitely more graphic. I leafed through the first few pages wondering why my brother and classmates so treasured these magazines. But then, in the final photo spread, I saw something. Something very exciting. Standing next to a naked woman was a naked man!

I quickly discovered the mechanics and pleasures of masturbation, and then masturbation's unpleasant sidekick—guilt. But guilt didn't stop me from indelibly etching the man's beautifully tanned physique into my memory to be replayed over and over and over again. My dormant fantasy life stood up and yelled "Whoopee!" as I daydreamed constantly of other boys and the man from the magazine.

There were other changes in my life as well. A concerted effort on my part, combined with the onset of puberty, led to a drastic change in my physical appearance. I grew two inches and lost 30 pounds the summer before my freshman year of high school. I looked and felt better than ever. With newfound confidence, I made friends and began participating in school activities. As my horizons expanded, my devotion to Believers' Chapel diminished. I no longer needed the sense of belonging the church had provided. But I had learned not to cross my father, so I continued to perform on Sundays, and I continued to participate in family Bible study.

Secretly, however, I looked forward to school and school events where I could spend time with my new friends. I had, at long last, ceased to be fat and boring. For the first time in my life, other kids actually invited me to do things with them. So when my father announced we would be moving to Muncie, Ind., I was devastated.

Monty had just graduated from high school and made up his mind to stay in Tennessee, but my mother, sisters, and I lacked this freedom. We argued against the move; Mother did not want to leave her family behind, and I did not want to leave my new friends. But, as it had been with our conversion to fundamentalist Christianity, our protests were futile. My father had already accepted a teaching position at Ball State University and, sight unseen, rented a house. The matter was settled.

After many days of moping, I began to see potential advantages to our move. No one at my new school would know what a fat sissy I had been. I sensed a prime opportunity to become a member of the "in" crowd and formulated a plan. As my mother and father prepared for our move, I worked odd jobs to finance the purchase of a new wardrobe. When I arrived in Muncie, I decided that my new classmates were going to see a skinny, handsome boy dressed in the latest designer sportswear.

"That looks like a scene from *Happy Days*," said Scott, now paying more attention to my photo album than his driving.

"I know," I answered. "That's my high school in Indiana. I loved it."

My father relocated us to Yorktown, a former farming community that had become a moderately affluent suburb of nearby Muncie. In Yorktown the homes were nestled among the Indiana trees, and everyone but us belonged to the country club. Murfreesboro faded to a drab, dreary memory.

Our new house sat on a nicely landscaped lot near the end of a cul-de-sac. Living in this new, well-to-do neighborhood made my family look wealthier than we really were, an illusion I happily reinforced by constantly wearing my new Izod shirts, matching socks, and Docksider shoes. I became friends with the most popular kids in school and found myself invited to parties, school dances, and lunch at the "cool" kids' table. My dream of being skinny and popular had finally come true.

Over the next two years, I became more involved with school and less involved with church. I attended services at our new church, of course, but activities like the Speech and Debate Club, the school play, and a part-time job at a candy store kept me away from home most evenings, limiting my participation in family Bible discussions. My father was less than thrilled, though Mother seemed pleased with my successes.

One morning during breakfast, my father expressed concern over my worldly activities. He announced that from then on I would be required to let him know my plans for the upcoming weekend each Monday so that he could spend the week praying for guidance. On Friday morning, he said, he would tell me if God approved. I choked down my cereal and opened my mouth to protest, but I refrained. He had been complaining for weeks about our new church, and I suspected he missed the control he'd had at Believers' Chapel. I knew that challenging his right to "communicate with God through prayer" would be a mistake. At the very least, it might have caused one of the already-bulging veins in his forehead to burst. I had an algebra exam that day, and a stroke over breakfast would have thrown me off my stride.

I realized that if I wanted to leave the house on a weekend, I had better produce some believable lies. I developed a habit of telling him that my friends and I planned to go to the early showing of a PG-rated movie—R movies weren't acceptable, and G movies weren't believable—and then for pizza. This would get me home by my 10 o'clock curfew. The only difficulty with this was making sure I knew the plot of whatever movie we were supposed to have seen in case someone questioned me.

I even began dating girls—not because I wanted to—but because my father would extend my curfew to 11 o'clock. Eleven still seemed early in comparison to when my friends had to be home, but it wasn't as embarrassing as 10 o'clock. And kissing a girl, not exactly repulsive but certainly not as exciting as I knew it was supposed to be, was a small price to pay for this extra hour of freedom.

My friends, along with the understanding girlfriends I kept as platonic as possible, accepted the explanation that my parents were religious and helped me scheme ways around my curfew—including a series of perilous late-night drops from my second-story window. Sneaking out was dangerous. Sneaking back in required death-defying feats rarely performed beyond the confines of a circus ring.

Week after week, I worried that my parents would catch me in a lie, that they would find out my friends and I had gone cruising or to a beer bash instead of to the movies to see *Footloose* for the 43rd time. But I was never caught—until the ill-fated "church retreat" that precipitated our move back to Murfreesboro.

After two years at tiny, suburban Yorktown High School, returning to Murfreesboro to attend a large county school, Riverdale High, was painful. In my absence the students had established cliques, walls of camaraderie I found difficult to breach.

Loneliness enhanced my sense of being different. I tried desperately to suppress my sexual attraction to men but failed. I began to equate terms like *gay* and *homosexual* to the feelings I experienced but had no confidante or role model to talk to or emulate. Even if I had, I probably would not have shared my secret.

I do have one happy memory of that year, my 18th birthday. I showed Scott pictures of the surprise party my parents threw for me. They invited members of the church and the few friends I had made since returning to Tennessee. I'd expected the usual shirt or pair of pants as a gift and was shocked when my normally staid father presented me with a framed poem he had written, "A Bouquet for Stuart." In

retrospect, the poem is a thinly disguised effort to turn me
into a "man," with lines such as:

> *How 'bout a fellow so handsome and groomed,*
> *He has all the young ladies around in a swoon?*
> *Yet modest he is about his good looks,*
> *But makes the Casanovas look like real*
> *schnooks.*

The poem praised me excessively in awkwardly metered
verse, ending with the lines:

> *Who is he, you ask, this fellow sounds fun,*
> *I tell you with pleasure, this fellow's my son.*

I had tears in my eyes as my father read the poem, not
from the beauty of the poem, but from joy that he felt that
way and sadness that he had never before praised me like
that. I had always believed he was ashamed of his dainty
purse-toting son. Did he really not care about my lack of
athletic and mechanical skills? I thought. I hoped the event
would mark a turning point in our relationship and resolved
to equal his poetic vision. I would make my father proud.

Mere months later, full of hope and good intentions, I
enrolled at the University of Tennessee, my father's under-
graduate alma mater. I attended classes regularly and stud-

ied earnestly. For a few weeks. But the specter of family and constraints of religion no longer existed. I had suddenly acquired freedom. I began to party, drinking excessively and using cocaine to hide my feelings of inadequacy, which were especially overwhelming when dealing with women. And they *were* women at UT. In high school I had dated girls—girls with "good personalities." Our evenings were easily limited to good-night kisses. Collegiate women expected me to be more aggressive, especially the women in the crowd I spent time with.

My grades and self-esteem plummeted, and after one "snowy" weekend, I knew I could not continue. I telephoned my mother, planning to confess everything—the drinking, my grades, the cocaine, and most of all my secret.

"Mama," I sobbed into the phone when as I heard her voice. She asked if I was all right.

"Please come get me," I pleaded. "I need to come home."

We spoke for 30 minutes, avoiding all I had planned to tell her. In the end we agreed I was homesick and that college classes were more difficult than expected. Everything was normal. Everything was fine.

I flunked out less than a month later. So much for making my father proud.

I crept back to Murfreesboro, tail between my legs, the image reminding me of that shame-filled childhood scene in which my brother and his friends had caught me with my penis tucked between my legs. My father welcomed me back but said if I planned to live in his house, he insisted on a few conditions. He produced a typewritten list: I would get a job; I would be home by 9 o'clock unless I was working; I would be in bed by 10 o'clock unless I was working; I would be up by 7 o'clock; I would eat all meals with the family; I would not drink or otherwise engage in immoral activities; I would perform an assigned list of daily chores.... The list went on and on.

I was penniless and had nowhere else to go, a tenuous bargaining position. I agreed to his terms. He instructed me to sign the paper, and I did.

I was humiliated but also motivated. I accepted a job managing a sporting-goods store and worked as many hours per week as I could. Within a few months I saved enough money to move into my own apartment, which I promptly did, much to my father's dismay.

I am certain he planned for me to take that step, just not so quickly. He wanted a little more time to teach me a lesson. But the man had spent years motivating unexceptional students, and his skills transferred nicely to the onerous task of jump-starting his teenage son. My few months at home were difficult, and I hated my father's tactics, but he forced me to mature and provided the impetus I needed to pull my life together.

I spent the next year living alone in my small apartment, throwing my energy into my job. As it had for Granddaddy and Nanny Howell, hard work paid off. I purchased a new car and lived comfortably. I also made a new best friend, Jeff. Tall, good-looking, and crazy about women, Jeff represented everything I had always wanted to be. He attended Middle Tennessee State University and encouraged me to return to school. I took his advice and plunged forward toward a degree in public relations.

Jeff belonged to Sigma Alpha Epsilon, the best fraternity on campus, and, again with his encouragement, I pledged during my first semester. Focused as I hadn't been at UT, I did well in classes and in the fraternity, earning excellent grades and holding a number of fraternal offices. Between work, school, and the house, I had no time to worry about my dark secret. As a senior, my brothers elected me president of the fraternity. I dated a beautiful sorority girl, Margaret, with whom I was surprisingly sexually active. Occasionally, I was able to reach orgasm without fantasizing about men. As far as I was concerned, the pudgy boy with no friends was nothing more than a distant memory.

I turned to a picture of Margaret and me at my fraternity's fall formal.

"She's pretty," Scott commented. I realized at that moment that she looked a lot like Scott. She could have been his sister.

It was about the time the photograph was taken that Margaret and I grew serious about our relationship. I knew I could never be completely happy with a woman but thought that with Margaret I had a chance to live a "normal" life. Something was missing, but I loved her. I still do. I convinced myself that love would be enough and decided to propose after spring break in Fort Lauderdale, Fla.

Several fraternity brothers, "little sisters," and I arrived in Fort Lauderdale after an exhausting 18-hour drive ready to party like we had never partied before. Mecca. We spent the week roaming from club to club, drinking and watching wet T-shirt contests. My fraternity brothers pursued woman after woman and tried to persuade me I should too. Margaret would never know, they said. I pleaded my impending engagement and refrained.

We started drinking early on the final day of our vacation, ending up more than a mile from our hotel at our favorite club, Summer's. Summer's looked like something from a movie—lit dance floor, swimming pool, sand volleyball courts in back, and booze, booze, booze. Shooters, shots, slammers: We drank them all. By midnight, I'd had enough. Drunk, drenched in beer and sticky drinks, I escaped out a side exit.

I found myself walking next to an attractive man. He asked where I was going and if I needed a ride. I thanked him for the offer, told him I was headed to my hotel, and accepted the lift. His had parked his red convertible around the corner and suggested, since it was such a nice evening, that we tour the city. He was in town on business from Seattle, he told me, and then, after more talking, he took my hand and placed it on his leg. We pulled over behind an abandoned shopping mall, and he kissed me. For the first time in my life, I felt sexually alive.

One brief encounter with a man I didn't even know erased 23 years of repression and denial. Despite "knowing" for many years that I desired men, it took this indiscriminate night to make me completely admit my homosexuality.

After he unceremoniously dumped me in my hotel's parking lot, I said aloud, for the first time, three little words: "I am gay." No one heard me, but I had taken an important step. I felt as if an incredible weight had been lifted from my chest. I had no immediate intention of spreading my news, but at least I was no longer lying to myself.

We returned to school, and I continued to see Margaret and participate in fraternity activities—to pass as straight—but I refrained from asking Margaret to marry me. And I added a new activity to my schedule, visiting Nashville's gay bars.

I had known of the establishments for about a year and had even driven past one several times. But like most gay bars in small cities, the windows were blacked out, and it looked abandoned. I'd never had the courage to go in. After my experience in Florida, however, I decided to check the place out.

I parked my car several blocks away and crept down a dark and dangerous side street to avoid being seen by anyone I might know. I scanned the street in front of the bar and, after watching several men enter, gathered my courage and went inside. Much to my surprise, I found myself in a crowded, lively bar packed with men, men, and more men. On my third visit I ran into one of my fraternity brothers, as well as a coworker, John, who later became my roommate and close friend. "Welcome to the club," John said.

As when Dorothy clicked the heels of her ruby slippers—once, twice, thrice—I was home.

After graduation I accepted a job with a television station in Huntsville, Ala., as promotions producer for the news department. Margaret had taken a job in Chicago, and I used our lack of physical proximity as an excuse to end our romance. Finally, free of encumbrances, I dived headfirst into the happy task of becoming the best homosexual I could possibly be.

As Scott and I neared the end our cross-country journey, I found the distance we had traveled symbolic of the relationship I had with my parents. By admitting I was gay, I had dug an emotional chasm, much as my move to California had created a geographical chasm. I closed the photo album as Scott and I entered Los Angeles, my exhaustion matched only by my fear of what might lie ahead.

CHAPTER 3

DECLARATION OF WAR

Steel. Glass. Sunshine. Downtown Los Angeles is the metropolis of my childhood dreams. A city! All people have a strong opinion about L.A. They either love it or hate it. I love it and can't imagine living anywhere else. Despite its many faults—earthquakes, riots, landslides, fires—it is my home.

I watched Scott lean over the steering wheel to get a better view of the palm trees lining the highway. Would he love L.A. or hate it? I wondered. I looked for a sign, attempting to gauge his reaction, but he gave no indication of his feelings—until we turned onto his new street, Alta Vista Boulevard. A big smile crossed his face as we pulled to the curb. He had heard much about our spacious window-laden apartment, rooftop pool, and tropical courtyard garden. He was on fire as we headed inside.

John met us at the door, a homemade banner, held between his outstretched arms, that read WELCOME HOME STUART AND SCOTT! The banner covered his face, but I knew well the cocky grin it concealed. He tossed the long paper aside, and we greeted each other properly, with bear hugs, then peppered one another with questions. "How was the trip?" "Did anyone call?" "Did you really come out to your parents?" "Is that my pile of mail?" "How did your parents react?" The easy questions were answered. The more difficult last question was put off.

I was pleased to hear that Andrew, my most recent ex-boyfriend, had called several times asking when I would be back in town. The mail, of course, was mine and looked to be nothing but bills. The phone company and credit card companies don't take vacations, even if their customers do. I decided to let the envelopes sit, along with John's question about my family's reaction. Our adrenaline would be better spent unloading the car than catching up.

We lugged Scott's possessions and my suitcases from the car to our third-floor home. The building's elevator spared our thighs, but my arms and shoulders screamed bloody murder. I made a mental note to either start working out or stop helping friends move. Scott and I collapsed in the living room amid boxes and suitcases and piles of clothing while the always-enterprising John prepared an ample batch of sweet tea. Central air and cold drinks—welcome to California.

As John poured our tea, I began to giggle, picturing the three of us as Charlie's Angels. With his James Caan looks and feisty demeanor, John would make a perfect Jaclyn Smith. The blond and sexy Scott was a dead ringer for Farrah Fawcett. And I would be the clever and crafty Kate Jackson. I explained my laughter, launching my roommates into a debate over whether Scott was better as Farrah Fawcett or cast latecomer Cheryl Ladd.

"Farrah," Scott pronounced with finality. "She had much better hair."

We began to relax, and John again asked how my parents had reacted to my news. Unloading the car had sapped what little energy I had left after the cross-country car ride, so I provided a condensed version. But for John, who had met my parents and not particularly cared for them, that was enough. He said little but sympathized, letting me know he was sorry my mother and father had reacted so poorly.

After finishing the pitcher of tea, we turned our attention to more mundane tasks. John and Scott unpacked Scott's belongings, chitchatted idly, and exchanged the latest gay gossip. I checked the messages on my answering machine, then sorted my pile of mail.

While separating the junk mail from the bills, and the bills requiring immediate attention from those that could wait, I encountered one personal letter—from my Aunt Brenda. I pushed aside the bills to read what I knew would be a supportive reply to the coming-out note I'd left. She and Uncle Ray had always been relatively progressive. I counted on them to sympathize and to help my parents accept my homosexuality. To me, this letter symbolized the beginning of my ascent from a deep pit of parental abandonment.

As it turned out, the pages were filled with vitriol and rancor from beginning to end. "I've heard that coming out of the closet is a 'cleansing' process. Well, aren't you selfish!" my aunt wrote. "You cleansed yourself, went back to your sweet little lifestyle, and left the rest of us to wallow in your sin!" She said she would never forgive me and that I should seek both Christian counseling and medical help. To make certain I understood, she added, "Did you really expect us to have compassion for you? I'm not Jesus!"

She closed by telling me she could no longer consider me a part of her family and that I should remember the price I had to pay for "choosing" my lifestyle. She signed the letter with her full name.

"Stuart, are you OK?"

"Stuart, what's wrong?"

I stared at the letter until John or Scott, I don't know which, took it. I went into the bathroom and shut the door—sick, dazed, stunned, awash in the words of my aunt. "There are certain feelings we have to suppress…I will never forgive you…You definitely have a hormonal imbalance…I can no longer consider you a part of my family."

I thought back to the many relaxed summer afternoons Brenda and I had spent poolside in her backyard drinking bourbon and sevens and gossiping. "Did I tell you about your Cousin Matthew's girlfriend?" "Don't tell me he lost another one." "Mmm hmm. Why don't you get us another drink?" I had always viewed her as a second mother. She and Uncle Ray had even given me $500 for college when my father wouldn't because I had "already flunked out."

Brenda and I had talked many times about my job as an AIDS educator. She was the only family member who expressed interest in what I did, the only one willing to even discuss the topic on more than a superficial level. I'd assumed she knew, at least subconsciously, that I was gay. After all, I had seen her defend gays.

She and my mother met me for lunch in Nashville one afternoon. They had been shopping. I'd spent the morning counseling a favorite client, an actor named Danny. I shared his story over our rabbitlike meal. Danny had never been tested for HIV, though he had been out and sexually active for many years. Consequently, he didn't find out he was HIV-positive until hospitalized, already suffering from AIDS. His parents, instead of supporting him, sent a letter telling him he had gotten what he deserved. "Like AIDS is some sort of punishment from God," I said.

"Well it is," responded my mother. Then she took a sip of her water and changed the subject, saying she didn't see how anyone could "drink water with a lemon in it." She spooned the yellow wedge from her glass and continued discussing lemons and water as if she hadn't a clue she had just horrified her son and sister. "If I wanted lemonade, I would have ordered it," she said. When she got no response, she realized she would have to elaborate. "The Bible is very clear about it. Homosexuals are going to hell."

"That's not true," I said.

"The Bible says a man shall not lie with another man as with a woman." She turned her attention back to her lemon, squeezing the waterlogged wedge over her salad.

Aunt Brenda intervened. "Toodie! I can't believe you. It might be a sin to be homosexual, but we all sin. I don't think homosexuals are going to hell any more than the rest of us." Then, after a pause, "Does this place have a dessert cart?" Aunt Brenda is more adept at changing topics than her sister, perhaps because she knows what to change the topic to: dessert. "I'm not going to get anything," she explained. "I just want to window-shop."

I reeled from the realization that Aunt Brenda wouldn't treat her much-favored nephew with the same compassion as his once-upon-a-time client, but I didn't want to ruin Scott's first day in California. I splashed water on my face, rejoined my roommates in the living room, and pretended to be over it.

"This is just an initial reaction," suggested Scott.

John agreed. "She's just mad because her sister's upset. You would be too. In a few days she'll realize your mom is wrong, and then she'll help you smooth things out."

I wanted to believe them so badly that I did. It was just an initial reaction. An apology had probably already been mailed. With that thought in mind, we headed out for a night on the town.

We walked the streets of West Hollywood, gay heaven, showing Scott the sights. Our first stop was Rage—Toto, I don't think we're in Kansas anymore!—a throbbingly loud, incredibly crowded dance club where John's boyfriend worked as a bartender. On my first visit I had been amazed by the windows. People could sit or stand or dance in full public view. Rage was a far cry from the blacked-out, boarded-up, windowless gay bars of the South. We downed several free drinks, courtesy of John's beau, before continuing our West Hollywood tour.

We popped in at Mickey's, then ambled to Revolver, my favorite bar. Revolver was a video bar with no dancing—an "S and M" bar, I explained to Scott.

"S and M?" he asked. "Like a leather bar?"

"No," I answered. "S and M like Stand and Model," which is precisely what we did for the remainder of the evening, Scott looking to impress the locals, me hoping Andrew would stop in. He didn't. Scott and John fared no better, probably because we left the bar well in advance of the last-call-mad-dash-for-a-date. We were tired and all needed to be up early the next day—John to work out, me to drive Scott to the airport so that he could catch a plane to New York for a gig he'd booked before moving, and Scott to catch the plane. Ah, the jet-setting life of an actor.

Scott hadn't bought furniture, so he slept in my room that night. It was the first time we had shared a bed since breaking up. I reread my aunt's letter before turning out the light. I didn't know where her hatred came from. She and Uncle Ray attended church only sporadically, and I couldn't remember their ever discussing religion, except for comments about my father's fanaticism. We had never passed a cross word, and I had always believed our relationship to be special and wonderful. I fought an onslaught of bewildered, angry tears. I wished Scott and I had never broken up, that he could hold me and comfort me. But that was impossible. We drifted off to sleep on the edges of my queen-size bed; three sets of lovers could have filled the space between us.

The next morning I rose early but had no time to contemplate family matters. I showered and dressed quickly (for me), yet still found Scott waiting impatiently by the door, tapping his foot. I rolled my eyes and led the way out. "We'll make it," I told him. "There won't be any traffic at this hour." A lie. Los Angeles thoroughfares are perpetually swarmed, no matter the hour.

The drive to the airport, however early and annoying, at least served a dual purpose. In addition to dropping off Scott, I was set to pick up my ex-girlfriend, Margaret, arriving on a red-eye from Chicago. Her trip had been planned for months, and I eagerly awaited her arrival. As Scott's plane taxied down one runway, Margaret's landed on another. Perfect timing.

As I waited for her to disembark, I thought back to the day I had told her the real reason we had broken up. She had been living in Chicago, and I hadn't seen her for several months when she decided to visit her family, and me, in Tennessee. As far as she knew, our three-year courtship had ended because I wasn't willing to engage in a long-distance relationship.

I had taken her with me for cocktails at the home of two well-off friends, longtime lovers named Lamar and Ray. Their living room was equipped with a baby grand piano, and Margaret and I were easily persuaded to perform. I plinked away and Margaret belted sappy love songs at the request of Lamar and Ray—*Memories*, *The Way We Were*, the theme from *Ice Castles*. No one mentioned that Margaret was the only straight person in the room, but the message all but screamed itself from the tastefully appointed surroundings.

The next night I took Margaret to a movie, dropping the obvious bomb on the way there. She admitted she knew, then asked if I was OK and if I'd told my parents. I answered her questions "Yes" and "No" respectively, and then we went in to watch the show. She'd always had gay friends, and I decided this must have eased the blow.

After that evening we didn't talk until she telephoned late one night. "Our whole relationship was a lie!" she screamed. "You used me! I was just some pretty little front for you so that you could be the big man on campus!"

Apparently she hadn't taken the news as well as I had thought. And what could I say to her when she was so obviously correct? Nothing, I decided, except the truth. "You're right," I answered. "But I really did love you. And I thought that was enough. I thought I could be straight if I just loved you enough." Unfortunately, she had heard too many lies to believe me and hung up. I hung up as well. No sense protesting to a dial tone.

We didn't speak again until the wedding of two mutual friends, a sorority sister of hers and a fraternity brother of mine. The happy couple had asked us to perform at the ceremony, and we couldn't let them down. Besides, if we said no, we would have to explain why. "I'm gay, and Margaret is mad at me because of it," and, "I dated a homosexual for three years, and I feel used," are interesting excuses, but not practical. Margaret and I talked a little while rehearsing, a little more at the wedding, and a little more afterward. Eventually we made up.

Standing in the airport in Los Angeles, I hoped my parents would come around as easily as Margaret.

She arrived exactly as expected, smile first, followed by her big blond hair and then the totality of her down-home allure. Living and performing in Chicago hadn't dimmed her girl-next-door sweetness one bit. She spotted me and waved, and I lamented my homosexuality, knowing that I loved this wonderful woman and always would. After a quick "Hey!" and a hug, Aunt Brenda's letter was forgotten.

In the car, though, Margaret reminded me by asking how my family was. This was her not-so-subtle method of asking if I'd come out to them. Like so many of my friends, she had been certain I would chicken out. As I weaved through early-morning rush-hour traffic I recounted the tale, closing with news of my aunt's letter. Margaret had gotten to know my family during our three years of courtship and sat in stunned disbelief.

"I just don't understand why people have to be this way," she said.

I pointed out landmarks, trying to change the subject.

Margaret ignored my efforts, one-track-minded as always. "Don't they realize you're the same person you've always been."

I shrugged.

"Ugh!" She slammed her fist on my dashboard. "Ugh! Ugh! Ugh!" She punctuated each "Ugh!" with another fist slam, each progressively harder than the one before.

When Margaret is mad everyone knows it.

Her temper fits are amusing if you're not the subject of her wrath. And even then her rage can be entertaining—in retrospect. When we were a couple, our pattern was to date for three or four months, break up, date for three or four months, break up, and so on. After our third or fourth breakup, Margaret had had enough. "Why do you do this to me?" she screamed. I sat in my recliner, the one noncollegiate piece of furniture in my very collegiate apartment, and coolly lit a cigarette. Her long blond hair had fallen into her face, so when she grabbed a pair of scissors from my nearby desk, she more than a little bit resembled Glenn Close in *Fatal Attraction*. Brandishing the scissors like a knife, she growled, "I'd like to kill you."

I smoked my cigarette, in no imminent peril. Margaret was dramatic, but not violent. I pointed to the bedroom. "You look tired," I said. "Why don't you go to bed? I'll sleep out here on the couch." She grunted, put down the scissors, and did as I'd suggested. I assumed the worst had passed.

Never, never, never assume with Margaret.

For the next hour I listened to hysterical wailing sobs. I tried everything not to hear them. I turned on the television. I turned on the stereo. I pressed pillows to my ears. I did all these things at once. But Margaret has a strong voice, a voice trained to carry across crowds of people, and nothing I attempted could drown her sorrow. Finally, I surrendered.

Not knowing what else to do, I went to the bedroom and asked if she wanted me to stay there with her. "Yes," she said. Then she snuffled, sniffled, snuffled again, and the crying jag was over. So, too, was the breakup.

After pounding my dashboard one last time, Margaret calmed and decided that after breakfast on the balcony we needed to spend the day on chaise lounges by the pool. She wanted to bronze herself in preparation for another long, cold Chicago winter. She agreed to cook, stretching the definition of "cook" with cold cereal and bagels, if I would mix a pitcher of Bloody Marys. "To start my vacation off right," she said.

Margaret fretted over my mother, of whom she had been fond, and asked if it might be OK to call her. We decided to wait a few days to see if Mother would call me first.

I was about to suggest we change into our bathing suits and reconvene by the pool for sunbathing and the remainder of the Bloody Marys when John returned from his morning workout carrying the day's mail. He held aloft a thick envelope, grinning like a child who has secretly opened, played with, and then carefully rewrapped all of his birthday presents. "It's from your parents," he announced.

"Open it!" clamored Margaret. "Open it!"

I did as ordered.

This wasn't a letter. It was a self-righteous, eight-page, typed, single-spaced rant. My father opened with a simple greeting, "Your visit was at first pleasant and then, unfortunately, it turned tragic." He told me he was shocked by my revelation, since he didn't think I was a homosexual. I wondered what he thought his purse-toting, rhinestone-earring-loving, sports-hating little boy was all those years. He wrote, "The Lord views men lying together as abominable and worthy of death." Then he referred to a Bible Pathways devotional booklet that talked about how the Christian must gently instruct those who are in opposition to the truth. "The Lord and I do not take kindly to our enemy slipping into the camp and stealing one of the sheep."

Then he launched into what can only be described as a declaration of war. "If you have never seen spiritual battle before, you are in for some of the roughest times of your life—as are we. This will not be stealthy jungle warfare but battle out in the open, exposing the forces of evil for who and what they are. Our battle plan will be public information, and you will be fully aware of every move. (If God is for us, who can stand against us?) One way or another you will be released, and God will be glorified."

Peppering his obsessive prose and twisted logic with words like "wickedness" and "abomination," my father told me that the punishment for a man lying with a man was death, but "since we don't live under a theocracy, we are not obliged to carry out the sentence." He attributed my escape from the noose to the fact that our legislators don't keep and enforce sodomy laws. He went on to say my passions weren't God's doing but were a result of the fall of man and that because of that the Lord expected me to resist. Since I had "merely dabbled" in the abomination, I could abstain from further acts and gain God's forgiveness. There was hope for me still.

After a lengthy diatribe on how the Lord saved sinners of his own acquaintance, my father reminded me that if I didn't change my ways I would become another of "the lost millions on a collision course with a Christless eternity."

He informed me that he had enlisted 27 "prayer warriors"—each named in the letter—to "join the brigade to petition the Father to rescue [me] from the enemy camp." They would not be praying for me to be saved, he said. Instead, they would ask the Lord to show me my salvation, to "woo" me, to "convince" me that homosexual acts were a sin and an abomination, to fill me and my "fellow sodomites with disgust" and "contempt" for our "deathstyle." He would ask the Lord to "strongly curse" those who had encouraged my sexual perversion and to drive an "irreversible wedge" between me "and others who advocate sodomy." Then, as if the Lord didn't have a monumental enough task on his hands, Dad and his prayer warriors planned to ask him to "thwart" my attempts to engage in perverted acts and to open my eyes to the fact that my orientation was merely a temptation, the product of a fallen world. The Lord would give me the strength to remain celibate in the face of my weakness of the flesh, my father wrote. And finally, the prayer warriors would ask God to "maintain unbearable pressure on me" until I sought him once again or, if I sinned unto death, until he took me.

Ever the professor, my father enclosed a flowchart outlining my options for life or death. "Like God," he wrote, "we want only the very best for you, but also like God we vehemently hate your sin. Today is the day of salvation. Turn to the Lord so that He will turn you from your sin."

The letter was signed, "In the love of Christ Jesus."

Margaret and then John had been picking up pages of the letter as I dropped them, reading along a few hundred words behind me. As I waited for them to finish, I pictured my mother in my father's messy study, wire-rimmed glasses perched on her nose, surrounded by her husband's scattered papers and cast-off 1960s furniture. She had steadfastly refused to use a computer and, until my gift of an electric typewriter a few years earlier, had pecked away on an aging relic, correcting her rare mistakes with correction fluid. I wondered if she believed the words she typed or if she merely transcribed my father's thoughts with no input and little comprehension as she had done with his dissertation so many years before—the perfect secretary, an automaton.

"I do not believe this," exclaimed Margaret when she finished reading the letter. "The man is insane!"

"He's convinced he's right," I said.

Margaret continued, picking up on what I later recognized as the main theme of his argument. "Your father actually believes God is going to kill you!"

"This is crazy!" John said, having finished as well.

I didn't agree with my father's views, but my inner child still accepted the urge to believe him, to obey him "or else."

"Are you OK?" Margaret asked as she stood to clear the breakfast dishes.

"Sit," I ordered. I felt even worse than I had the day I came out to my parents, but I didn't cry. Perhaps the events of the previous week had hardened me, or perhaps my well of tears had temporarily run dry. "I'm fine," I continued. "I'm going to put this letter away and forget about it for a while. When things calm down, I'll take another look."

Margaret debated internally, then sat back down. She dipped her fingers into her drink and flicked them in my direction, spraying me with tomato-sticky droplets. Then she stuck out her tongue and gave me the raspberry. *Phhblllttt!* I love Margaret. I really do.

I remember little of the next week except that Larry, a friend I'd had a weeklong fling with in Washington, D.C., the month before, unexpectedly decided to visit. So now I had two houseguests with whom I'd been romantically involved. Unfortunately, the spark with Larry had flickered. The situation proved to be more awkward than romantic.

With no alternative, I did exactly what I'd told Margaret I would do. I put my father's letter away and forgot about it for a few days. For the remainder of my houseguests' stay, I was a tourist.

After Larry and Margaret departed, I took a few days and settled back into my routine before rereading my father's letter. Then I wrote my angry, yet honest reply.

September 15, 1992

Dear Dad,

I am writing in response to the letter you sent last week. Since Mother did not sign the letter, I am not sure she agrees with all you said. However, I hope you will share this response with her.

Our disagreements in many areas are so large that it is difficult to know where to begin. Until now, I didn't think that it was so important for you to know my views on several subjects. Many of the issues brought up in your letter have caused me to change my mind.

First of all, I feel that your letter was full of judgment. You have spent my lifetime trying to tell me what a Christian is or what the Bible says. You have never said "In my opinion" or "I believe it says this." Instead you have said "this is what it says." With so many learned and intelligent

*Christian scholars (many fundamentalists like yourself)
who cannot agree on what the Bible says, I find it funny
that you know for certain what it says and means. I find it
even more disheartening that you feel God has given you
the authority to judge my friends as "false counselors."*

*Let me take a moment and tell you about these so-called
false counselors. They are a very mixed group: heterosexual and homosexual; old and young; male and female;
Christian and Jewish. What they all have in common is love
and compassion. I have watched as they showed love to
people with AIDS, the homeless, drug users, and other
"sinners" who I have never witnessed you, Mother, or anyone from your "body of believers" even look twice at. They
have shown me an unselfish, nonjudgmental love that truly
represents what God means to me.*

*What have I seen as my Christian example at home? I
have seen judgmentalism and bigotry. I have watched as you
have hurt your children, other members of your family, and
your church with your judgments and piousness. I have listened to you postulate that you know the only way to have a
relationship with God. I have watched as you alienated family and friends. And finally, I have watched as you have become more miserable and unhappy with your job, where you
live, and your church. Is this what Christianity is to you?
Perhaps you should read what Christ says about the Phar-
isees. If I were to judge you, I would have to say that you do*

not represent the Christian that I believe God speaks of in the Bible. But I'm not called to judge you. Only you are responsible for your relationship with God, as am I for mine.

If we were Jewish, you would tell me that Christ was not the Messiah, and you would have biblical basis for your belief. If we were Catholic, you would tell me that there were extra books to the "inspired word of God" and you would have biblical basis for that. If we were Mormon, you would tell me that there was an extra book that was also a bible and you would have a biblical basis for that. Some of these people might call you a false counselor for not believing as they do. I wonder what God must think of all these people who believe they have all the answers. How arrogant! I choose to believe that all of these people can be right, that God is much more concerned with our hearts and souls than anything else.

I am not a theologian, so I won't even attempt to get into that discussion. However, if you want to pursue that path, I have many friends in Nashville (some even ordained ministers) who would be more than willing to discuss it with you. What I can tell you is how I try to live my life. I try to love God, my family, friends and the world—that's it! I try not to judge people (which I don't always succeed at), to instead worry about my own relationship with God, letting Him worry about everybody else. That is all I have ever expected from you or Mom. If you do something or believe something that I don't agree with—which is often—it doesn't matter because I am not called to be your conscience or your judge. I am called to love you, and I also try to be as supportive as possible.

As to telling you that I'm gay, I may not have told you in the most perfect way (if there is such a thing). However, I told you because it is who I am, and I will not hide my life any longer from people who supposedly love me unconditionally. From the time I was a little boy, I knew that I was attracted to other boys. I suppressed this for many years—dating women, having sex with women, and praying that I would grow out of it. I didn't and I'm glad! I told you because I love myself, who I am, and what I stand for. I told you because I love you and want you in my life. However, my life is a gay one. I told you because I believe that God made me this way, and like all things, he made me this way for a reason. I told you because I'm an adult and I won't live my life a certain way just to please you.

I am very blessed to have so many wonderful friends that I have adopted as members of my family. These are people who have stood by me through thick and thin and prove to me every day what God's love is all about. They don't all agree that homosexuality is right, but they don't find it necessary to judge me. You say these friendships won't last. All I can say is that they have lasted for years and have provided more love and support than I have ever felt from you. God has blessed me with a full, rich, rewarding, and happy life. I hope that your life is the same.

Mother has told me several times that you do not understand why your sons are not close to you or why you don't have friends. Is it Christ's plan for you to be isolated? Or could it be that perhaps you are the root of the problem? Monty and I are as different as night and day but share very similar feelings about you. I am sorry if this is hurtful, Dad, but feel that it is time for me to be brutally honest. Please take a long look at yourself and think about your life before it is too late.

You know very little of me or my life, Dad, and yet are able to fill pages judging it. Why don't you try to get to know me. I do want my family, but not at the cost of losing myself. I'm not going to give up my beliefs simply to make it easier for you or Mom. I am sorry if I've hurt you or Mom, but I must say, I've done my share of hurting too, and with no out-stretched hand from either one of you. I have been a good, loving son, led a productive life helping others, and am happy. I would think that this would make any parent happy.

I hope that someday we will be able to look back on this with a deeper understanding and love for one another. I am praying for you as I have requested my friends to do also. I do love you and Mother.

Your son,

Stuart

P.S. I have enclosed a copy of Brenda's letter to me and am forwarding a copy of it, your letter, and this letter to Monty and Barbara.

For possibly only the second time in my life, but certainly the second time in just a few weeks, I told the complete truth to my father.

I understood my father really believed—and still does—that homosexuality is a mortal sin and that his actions were an effort to save my soul. He may even believe his entreaties to God are the only reason I'm alive today. After all, this is a man who prays for a parking space before going to the grocery store and then praises the attentiveness and benevolence of God if he gets a space near the entrance.

On the topic of prayer, several of my friends did agree to pray for my father's enlightenment as I requested, though I doubt any have pursued this task as adamantly as my father and his prayer warriors. Several of these friends asked, begged even, for permission to write to my parents to express their feelings of outrage. But out of a sense of duty to my family—family business is family business—I requested that they refrain.

I now regret that decision since my father has ignored this sense of propriety, much as I do now by writing this memoir. Nevertheless, with my blunt answer to my father's horrific letter, the prayer war had begun in earnest.

CHAPTER 4

THE EXPANDING FRONT

Saturday morning. Quiet. Scott was in New York, and John was away for the weekend with his boyfriend. I was alone for the first time in more than a month. Disoriented, frightened, determined, I started a pot of coffee. I popped a Marianne Williamson tape into the stereo and settled into a "me" day. I melted into my favorite chair and listened to Marianne's message of forgiveness and its necessary place in our lives—forgiveness of those who have hurt us and, more importantly, forgiveness of ourselves.

I had discovered Marianne Williamson through a friend and coworker, Chaz, a middle-aged, pleasantly plump Latino from northern California. Chaz is a "sparkler," a person who can walk into a crowded room and within minutes be on a first- name basis with everyone, making jokes, sharing

secrets, inviting them to dinner. He is the person I connected with when I started work at the Gay and Lesbian Center. I showed up my first day, a lonely boy from Tennessee,
scared, questioning my decision. Chaz took me under his
wing, showed me around, introduced me, gave me coffee,
and made me laugh and feel comfortable.

On the surface, Chaz and I could not be more different,
but we found ourselves connecting on a deep level through
our respective searches for spiritual enlightenment. As a
young man, Chaz had rejected his Catholic upbringing,
choosing instead to attend seminary at a Baptist College.
He served as a Baptist minister in Texas but found the fundamentalist movement incompatible with his inner self. He
left the church, moving to a straight marriage and corporate
America. By his late 30s he had moved to Los Angeles,
come out, and begun his search for truth.

Not long after we met, Chaz suggested I listen to a tape
of Marianne Williamson. "She'll change your life," he told
me. I borrowed one of his collection of tapes and quickly
got hooked. Williamson struck me as a real person, talking
about real issues, offering real solutions—a huge change
from the static dogma I'd been force-fed since childhood.

Her teachings come primarily from *A Course in Miracles*, a book written in the 1960s. She also draws on the
universal truths found in nearly all religious and spiritual
teachings, most notably the need to love and be loved.

What was so refreshing to me was that she didn't talk about "bad" people and the need to be saved. She talked about "good" people and the need to express goodness through love—of yourself and those around you.

✳ Through her I learned the fear I had been taught from infancy was really a fear of love, a self-imposed fear that sometimes causes individuals to embrace traditional religions like fundamentalist Christianity, religions that provide solace through the definition and prohibition of taboo acts. Taboo, depending on the religion, can be anything from premarital sex, to alcohol, to birth control, to killing cows, to homosexuality. The most unfortunate part of this fear of love is that individuals who give in to it often coerce innocents like me, my mother, my brother, and my sisters into following their rocky path.

Before I heard Marianne Williamson, I thought all religions relied on emotional self-mutilation. In my mind, religion was an all-or-nothing proposition. And the "all" told me I was evil, a sinner, doomed for eternity.

I soon borrowed the remainder of Chaz's Marianne Williamson tape collection. After years of bitter medicine, her message slid down like a spoonful of sugar. I devoured it, voracious, thrilled with the knowledge that my lifelong desire for spirituality based on love not only existed but also was being embraced by scores of people.

But those people weren't with me that Saturday morning. Neither were my roommates nor Marianne Williamson.

Loneliness consumed me. I stared at the wall and listened to her strong, throaty voice. "Forgive your brother," she said.

"Forgive your brother," I echoed. The phrase sounded weak when I said it, hollow, uttered not with my voice but with the reedy pipings of a forlorn child.

"Forgive your brother," Marianne repeated, relentless with her message.

I turned off the tape.

How could I forgive my family? How could I forgive the family that adored me until I refused to live by their rules? How could I forgive the family that reneged on its promise to love me unconditionally and forever? How could I forgive the family that placed the sanctity of a book above the well-being of their son?

To escape the silence I pulled back the curtains, opened the patio door, stepped onto the balcony, and gazed at the Hollywood Hills. The clear September morning seemed alive, clean, crisp, like Tennessee in early fall—perfect for football, raking leaves, or curling up with a book. My sprinkling of tears became a shower, a downpour, a hurricane.

Several hours later, curled in a ball in the corner of my living room, I drifted back to reality, to the smell of boiled-down coffee. All of the life had been drained from my body. I stumbled to the bathroom, glimpsed myself in the mirror, and recoiled in horror. My eyes were swollen and red, my hair looked as if I'd combed it with a Cuisinart.

I sat on the edge of the bathtub and prayed with feeling for the first time in years. "Please God, help me. Help me through this." And then more specifically, "Help me to love myself and to love my family."

My prayers worked—on my mood at least. Misery gave way to inner peace.

Marianne was right: "Forgive your brother."

I wandered to the kitchen and tricked myself into believing the black muck bubbling in my coffee maker was coffee and not goo from the La Brea Tar Pits. I diluted a cup of the viscous concoction with milk and sugar, much as my tears had diluted years of homophobia-related anger and frustration.

That evening my ex-boyfriend Andrew came over for dinner. An aspiring actor and naturally flirtatious, he knew everyone who was anyone in West Hollywood; I'd been flattered that he wanted a simple boy from Tennessee. We'd dated for three months, and I wasn't quite over him.

Like Chaz and me, Andrew and I couldn't have been more different. Still, we got along well, especially while dating. I provided a sense of security he hadn't encountered in his scores of romantic conquests, and he altered my Puritan-like view of sex. The only fights we'd had centered on my Ozzie and Harriet mind-set—sex should be clean, quiet, and never, ever discussed. Andrew felt differently. Much differently. Once, in the heat of passion, he demanded that I talk dirty to him. I steeled myself and tried to say something sexy in my best Jeff Stryker voice. But all that came out was laughter. The moment was lost, as was our relationship. *C'est la vie.*

Andrew and I talked over a meal of fat-free bean burritos and salad. He was anxious to read for himself the horrors I had described, so after dinner I supplied him with my aunt's and my father's letters.

Andrew read in silence, grinding his teeth. Then he exploded. He slammed the papers onto the counter and shouted, "Give me their addresses! I'll tell them what I think about their God!"

Andrew's anger nearly sent me into a fresh episode of crying. And after the day I'd had, another round of tears would have resulted in dehydration. He backed off, sensing more anger was the last thing I needed. He spent the remainder of the evening holding me. Cuddling was never his strong suit, but he did it perfectly that night.

The following week, life returned to normal. Scott and John reappeared, and I went back to work. The never-boring, never-dreary Gay and Lesbian Center had been the focus of my life since moving to Los Angeles, and the chaotic activities of my surrogate family provided welcome relief from the harsh reality of my biological family. Yet even in the midst of planning an upcoming fund-raiser, the rift between my parents and me gnawed nastily on my nerves.

Apparently the strain showed. My coworkers, the world's ultimate support group, outed my problems at a staff meeting and encouraged me, as my friend John had done in Nashville, to accept my own advice.

One of the programs I managed for the center was designed to build self-esteem among gay men so that they will practice or continue to practice safer sex. This was accomplished through group sessions in which participants discussed the effects of homophobia, both internal and external. My position as moderator enabled me to see and experience vicariously the pain of others, but it never forced me to deal with my own issues. Being a "fixer" that offered consolation and advice had allowed me to escape the self-examination I needed. What once had been a theoretical application of my interpersonal skills had now become an intrapersonal reality. I did, indeed, need a dose of my own medicine.

Planning a large fund-raiser on short notice and alternately suppressing and releasing deep-rooted anger and fear created a new category in "Weeks From Hell." I understood for the first time how some gay men subconsciously want to be infected with HIV. For them it is a way to ignore the ongoing, ordinary, day-to-day pain of living. If you have one huge, potentially insurmountable problem, then your other difficulties diminish.

Faulty logic? Absolutely. But enticing nonetheless.

I remember an intelligent and philosophical friend from high school in Indiana who would sit in class, nonplussed, while other students asked question after question about material he understood implicitly. "You must be bored," I would say. But he would deny it, explaining that without varying degrees of intelligence, he wouldn't be any smarter or any different than anyone else. Then, to illustrate his point, he would apply his logic to virtually any quality even remotely important to us at the time—physical beauty, athleticism, personality, ability to chug beer without throwing up...

Arriving home on Friday night of my Week from Hell to be greeted by the smell of one of Scott's delicious home-cooked meals is, I suppose, an extension of my high school friend's theory. For it was the pleasantness of this meal that made me realize how awful the previous seven days had been. I didn't realize how unhappy I'd been until something came along and made me happy.

Scott had spent two summers as a houseboy on Fire Island. He worked for a wealthy and generous couple who gave him the run of their beachside home, only showing up themselves on weekends. Scott's lone duty was to cook for them. He took his job seriously, studying high-priced cookbooks, watching cooking shows on cable television, and shopping at local markets for the freshest, tastiest ingredients. He spent his weekdays sunning and experimenting with recipes and his weekends astonishing his employers and their guests with his culinary skill, a rival to Wolfgang Puck.

Interestingly, the extension of my friend's theory works in both directions. You don't realize how good things are, like the dinner Scott was cooking, until something unpleasant comes along, like the letter from my father resting on top of the day's mail.

Dad's letter opened with Hebrews 4:12. "The Word of God is living and active and sharper than any two-edged sword, and piercing as far as the division of soul and spirit, of both joints and marrow." He castigated me for my "savage, reviling reaction" to his earlier letter. He said he had written his initial letter from "a loving, reconciliatory motive" and was disturbed that I had clearly not read it. Now that I had purged the venom from my system, he said, he was waiting for the circumspect response he deserved. In the meantime, he had enlisted 12 prayer warrior couples to pray for me. He suggested I await the fruits of their labor.

Scott and John watched as I read the letter and then placed it back in its envelope. "Another love note from home," I said. I tossed the letter onto the counter and Scott gave me a look indicating he had seen the return address when he carried in the mail, probably the motive behind his sudden desire to cook. John grabbed the letter, dropping the spoon he had been using to stir the sauce, to the obvious relief of Scott, who hates people messing with his concoctions.

I should have expected this response, but hadn't, and was shaken by my father's lack of compassion. This was not a loving response from a father and Christian—it was a declaration of war. "I shall initiate phase two of the reconciliation strategy..." What then? The atom bomb?

Furious, John broke the tension. "Who in the hell does he think he is?" He slammed the letter back to the counter, then mocked my father. "You have obviously not read my letter." Then he exploded once again. "He's nuts! We all read his damn letter. He just can't accept the fact that you won't do what he says."

I love it when John gets angry. He's almost as much fun as Margaret. Unfortunately, I was in no mood for his antics. I *had* read my father's letter. Over and over and over. And I had responded as honestly as I knew how. It hurt that he had ignored the father-son relationship issues I'd raised and retreated to his role as fundamentalist dictator, marshaling his troops, spewing rhetoric, preparing to attack.

For the next two weeks, I woke up early and spent an hour meditating, praying, and listening to tapes of Marianne Williamson before starting my day. Desperate, I sought answers from a God I wanted to believe in, a God that could solve all my problems. But the solutions were not forthcoming. My faith was tested, and my spirits fell.

Friends and coworkers, unable to fathom my parents' reaction, encouraged me to wait and see. "Things will change

in time," they told me. What they meant was "time heals."
But what I heard was "time will make things even worse."
They couldn't have known I would take their well-intentioned advice as poorly as I did. They didn't grow up in a
fundamentalist household. They didn't know that a fundamentalist Christian will cut off his arm if he believes it's
God will. And that's the situation I felt I was in. I had become an appendage, a rotting limb to be healed or ampu-
tated. And healing was not an option. I saw little hope.

To illustrate, I ask you to forget for a moment that my
parents truly believed they were doing the right thing, that
they honestly believed the consequences of going against
the "true" teachings of the Bible were death and eternal
damnation. Remember only that they outed me to their
church, their neighbors, and their family and friends. They
enlisted a prayer brigade to "save" me. Even if they wanted to change their beliefs and attitudes, they couldn't. My
parents painted themselves into a corner. They had placed
themselves in the position of accepting me as a gay son or
risking everything else that mattered in their world.

I foundered in my search for the best way to handle the situation. None of the coming-out books I'd read covered what
to do when your father and his church declare war on your
soul. None of my friends had experienced anything similar.

I chose to forget my father for a moment and to try to
reach my mother instead. My father had always been cool,

rigid, and emotionless, while Mother had always been warm, accepting, and loving. Furthermore, even though my father had a Ph.D. and Mother never finished college, I'd always believed she was the smarter of the two. She was the one who knew how to connect with people and make them feel special. Perhaps, I thought, my mother would seize the day. Perhaps she would step to the fore and save her family, even though taking a lead role rubbed against the grain of her entire life experience.

Mother grew up a middle child, sandwiched between a rambunctious older brother and a prettier, slightly spoiled younger sister. Like many middle children she became a background player, the family peacemaker. She carried her childhood role into adulthood and marriage, serving as the mediator who kept father and sons, brother and brother, and later sister and sister from strangling each other. The family ambassador. I saw greatness in her ability to hold us together. And it was this greatness, this intelligence and ability to play peacemaker, that I hoped to reach.

I sat at my desk and struggled to compose a letter. But before I had written even a single word, two letters arrived, one from my mother, the other from my youngest sister, Abby. I opened Mother's first, hoping the qualities I so much admired had surfaced on their own, that she had not really agreed with my father and would seek to make amends.

Mom's letter began innocuously: family events, my sisters' grades, Amy's upcoming class trip to Washington D.C., a planned visit by Grandaddy and Nanny Howell. Then she told me that she and Dad had finally shared my announcement with my sisters and that Amy and Abby agreed my lifestyle was sinful. Mother said that just days before telling my sisters, Amy had been watching *Little House on the Prairie* and commented that in *Little House* days they probably hanged gays. Mother told me that Abby was angry and disappointed in me and feeling very sad.

Mom said she was concerned not only with my spiritual well-being but also my physical health. She quoted an alleged American Psychological Association study, clipped from an unnamed magazine and taped to her letter, claiming the average gay man had 50 sexual partners a year—a statistic that painted me as woefully below average. That was why, according to the article, the Little Rock Lothario (a.k.a. Bill Clinton) felt so comfortable supporting the homosexual agenda.

Mom closed by saying that she loved me and that she prayed every day that I would reject my lifestyle and return home.

I imagined my mother writing this letter, seated in a straight-backed oak chair at our round kitchen table, a Bic pen pulled from her purse, a pad of yellow, blue-lined legal paper in front of her. She paid bills at this table, drank iced tea, gossiped with her sister, fed her family. It must have taken a great deal of love to sit at that table and inform me of family doings and caution me with well-intentioned misin-formation about what she had been taught to believe was a choice I'd made.

Abby's letter, written on little-girl stationery, was more painful to read than Mom's. She began by letting me know that Mom and Dad had told her I was gay. She said she loved me but that I had hurt her deeply. She thought I was selfish for hurting my family so much. She said, "I used to look up to you, but that's all changed now." Then she wrote of God's wrath. "He can either change you or kill you."

I couldn't understand where her anger came from. Abby and I had always been so close. I was 15 when she was born. I changed her diapers, fed her, and took her with me whenev-er I could. Sometimes I would even lie when people asked if she was my daughter and say she was—that was our little se-cret, even if Abby wasn't old enough to understand the joke.

So if my father's letters hurt, and my mother's letter hurt, Abby's nearly killed me. She wasn't supposed to side with my parents. I'd always thought she was too smart to accept their fundamentalist ravings.

I had to remind myself that she was only a child, 12 years old. Children can't overcome biases they are force-fed from birth. I certainly hadn't. I was well into my teens before I began to question my parents' ideology and into my 20s before I was able to independently and confidently reject it. So even if Abby believed she had reached her conclusions on her own, I knew she hadn't. That was my only solace.

On countless occasions my father had delivered to my brother, my sisters, and me a select collection of Bible verses and then left us alone to decide for ourselves what was right and what was wrong. He never allowed for the fact that there may have been opposing scriptural arguments. My father's version of spiritual education was tantamount to brainwashing. The following hypothetical provides an example. If an individual who has spent his entire life in a tiny room devoid of color is given a piece of red paper and told the color is blue, he will believe that red is really blue. If you then present him with a ripened apple, he will tell you it is blue and will honestly believe he has reached that conclusion on his own. I attribute Abby's sentiments regarding my homosexuality to this theory. She received one-sided and dubious information, and decided her brother was a blue fruit. (Pun intended.)

To hell with not answering my father. In the space of 30 minutes, I wrote the following letter.

October 4, 1992

Dad,

I just received a letter from Abby. Here's a quote: "God loves you very much. He can either change you or kill you." You have done a wonderful job instilling your message of hatred in your innocent twelve-year-old daughter. Congratulations!

As for letters, this will be my last to you for a while. I am not going to go back and forth with you. I hope that you have not deluded yourself so much that you actually believe your letters to me have been based out of love. Your letters and their language have been based on control, power, and manipulation. I will no longer allow you to manipulate me, although you are a master at it. The most frightening part is that you use God as your tool.

How totally arrogant of you to say, "So now that you have this venomous reaction out of your system and all is forgiven, I am waiting for the circumspect response that my letter deserves." First of all, I didn't ask you for forgiveness because I have done nothing but speak the truth as I see it. Second, as to the response your letter deserves, I'll leave that to you and God.

As to reading your initial letter, rest assured that I did, several times, line by line. It was much less a letter than a sermon, which seems to be the only way you have ever been able to communicate.

As to theology, I told you that I would not debate. I did, however, share your letter with several Bible scholars. They informed me that your interpretations were very biased. I quote one scholar: "His exegesis is limited in information and unskilled in technique. Any second-year Greek scholar could easily refute his one-sided arguments." Again, I extend my offer to you to meet with one of the theologians. Or would that disrupt the isolated, comfortable world where you are always right?

I wish you could have your beliefs and allow others to have theirs without judgment or condemnation, but for some reason, you and the rest of the family-values Christians have decided to be judge and jury. How fitting that Phyllis Schafley's son announced his homosexuality a few weeks ago, that Jerry Falwell's ministry faces bankruptcy, and that Oral Roberts's oldest son was supposedly gay and committed suicide—not to mention the foibles of Jimmy Swaggart and Jim Bakker. Why have these people fallen? Is it because they aren't good Christians? Is it because they chose to judge others?

You know, it's funny. All of my friends have been amazed at my peace and serenity during all of this. I do feel peace because I am comfortable for the first time in my life. I love myself regardless of your beliefs or opinions. God has blessed me, and I believe He has a hand in all of this. I believe that your reaction would have been just as strong had I announced I was converting to Judaism, Catholicism, or Mormonism. The only difference is that I didn't choose to be gay. I was born this way. No one made me turn gay and, quite frankly, I am very glad that I am gay. Some gay people would take a pill if it would make them straight. I wouldn't.

Dad, this is me, and nothing's going to change just because you want it to. I certainly don't believe that God wants me to change. I am a happy, loving, fulfilled, successful person. Take care of yourself and please leave my relationship with God between God and me.

Stuart

After writing the letter I put it aside, as I always do with letters, to be mailed the next day. I like to sleep on things to make sure I haven't said something I didn't mean—an outgrowth of my father's adage, "Never put anything in writing that you wouldn't want repeated." I did, however, intend to send the letter—until the Marianne Williamson lecture I attended that evening.

She spoke at a large Los Angeles theater packed with an eclectic crowd of Hollywood power brokers, housewives, 7-11 clerks, and gay men. Scores of gay men. I think homosexuals are drawn to her salty approach toward spirituality. Or maybe she's just another in a long line of divas—Maria Callas, RuPaul, Marianne Williamson...

After intermission Marianne took questions from the audience. I didn't raise my hand, though I did think about it. The first few queries were typical, "My boyfriend left me and blah, blah, blah," "My boss is a jerk and blah, blah, blah." And then a young man stood and spoke about his overbearing, toxic parents. I leaned forward in my seat; he could have been talking about my father.

"Wait a minute," shouted Marianne, stopping the man mid sentence. "Chemicals are toxic, not people." She scolded the man for dehumanizing his parents. "You've made them into robots," she said, "so you can dissect them without concern for their emotions or spiritual well-being." Her words might as well have been directed at me as the unfortunate soul a few rows away. "Parents are people," she said, "with feelings and problems of their own. To place the blame for your own unhappiness on them is unfair."

Had I done this to my father? Had I turned him into a walking, talking, pull-my-string-and-I'll-preach-at-you doll? Did I make my father inhuman so that I could blame him for the pain in my life without worrying or caring about his feelings?

What a drag. Just when you think you've found a villain, some obnoxiously practical person like Marianne Williamson comes along and ruins it.

Marianne's lesson of forgiveness echoed in my head all night . Forgiveness. The word is used often but seldom un-derstood. We forgive people for bumping into us at the su-permarket, for cutting us off on the freeway, even for end-ing a relationship because it "just didn't feel right." But when it comes to the real test of forgiveness, applying the feeling to those we love, most of us fail. This is because the people we are closest to are able to wound us the most deeply, and the more we hurt, the less likely we are to forgive—a classic catch-22.

Again I prayed. "God, help me to forgive. Teach me what forgiveness means. Show me how to love again." I drifted to sleep feeling as light as air, secure in the knowledge that God had heard my plea, that God would help me. The letter was never mailed.

I spent the next few weeks forgiving, forgiving, and forgiving some more. I forgave everyone for everything. I forgave anyone who had ever crossed me. And for those who hadn't crossed me, I conjured transgressions and forgave them too. All the while I hoped my parents were going through the same process, that without a response to their letters they would search their souls and realize the whole situation was just an initial knee-jerk reaction to learning their son was gay. After all, I decided, it had taken me years to come to grips with my homosexuality. Surely I could give my parents more than two short months.

So I waited for the love that was rightfully mine. Patiently I waited. And then it was Halloween, the world's finest excuse for dressing in drag.

West Hollywood buzzed with preparations for its gala event, the infamous Parade of Costumes. My roommates and I planned to attend a few cocktail parties and watch the show from a nearby street corner. West Hollywood neophytes, we had never seen anything even remotely like what our friends described. We felt like virgins on prom night, anxiously awaiting our inevitable deflowerings. We mixed drinks and watched one otherwise manly neighbor spend hours sewing glitter beads to a flowing purple muumuu. We were agog.

Konnnngggggg!

That is the sound of an anvil landing on my head, which would have been preferable to receiving another letter from Tennessee the day before Halloween. For professing to be so godly, fundamentalists have a decidedly ungodly sense of timing. Just when you're having fun... This one was from the pastor of Believers' Chapel, Brother Ken, Mary Lee's husband. I had always liked Ken, though as a boy his masculinity frightened me, probably the result of my own lack thereof. He had been a highway patrolman before becoming a minister, and his sermons were fascinating mixtures of rural law enforcement and fundamentalist theology, a cross between *In the Heat of the Night* and *The 700 Club*.

The letter surprised me. My father had told me that Brother Ken and Mary Lee would be enlisted as prayer warriors, but I hadn't expected to hear from them. I opened the envelope, expecting a tiny, sweaty Jerry Falwell to pop out ranting about salvation and the kingdoms of heaven and hell. I found instead a typed note.

Ken began his letter by telling me he didn't want to judge me before hearing both sides of the story. Then he proceeded to judge me. "Such a lifestyle is, short and simple, sin," he said. Any effort to paint my life in another way was useless. After beating around the bush for a paragraph, he fell into the exhausted arms of Leviticus: "If a man lies with a male as he lies with a woman, both of them have committed an abomination. They shall surely be put to death. Their blood shall be upon them." Ken closed by saying that even though he disapproved of my actions, he wouldn't turn me away and that he was praying for me.

I love it when people say, "I really need to hear both sides of the story before passing judgment but..." I've experienced a lot of this in my lifetime. In fact, I can honestly say I've never known a single fundamentalist Christian capable of waiting until you finish uttering a sentence, let alone a complete presentation of your side of the story, before passing judgment. Even so, it disappointed me that Ken didn't wait to hear my arguments. If he had, and had he acknowledged their relevance, and then brought forth his own arguments, he would have had a much greater chance of reaching me with his message. But Ken, fortunately or unfortunately, chose to judge my motives and behaviors based on secondhand knowledge of one and no knowledge of the other. I found it ironic that everyone disapproved of what I was doing when I'd never discussed what I'd done. I simply told them I was gay. I never mentioned sexual encounters, or if I'd even had one.

The pastor had opened his letter by quoting Proverbs: "He who answers a matter before he hears it, it is folly and shame to him." Well, shame on you, Brother Ken.

It irks me that when people are known to be heterosexual, no one thinks of anything more sinister than marriage and children. Let someone mention they're homosexual, however, and immediately the listener conjures images of illicit sex, anal fornication, and debauchery of all types. There is no thought about a man loving another man, only of a man having sex with another man. Even in the narrow Believers' Chapel interpretation of the Bible, loving another man is not a sin. All that is sin is the homosexual act. My family and my church judged me for actions they didn't even bother to ask if I'd performed. My anger on the topic wanes with the sheepish admission that their assumptions, though unproven, were correct. Still, I wonder if my parents would have become so incensed if the sex they assumed I'd had was with Margaret instead of a man. I wonder if they would have started their prayer war.

After several hours of moping, I put the letter away to be answered at a later date. Then I stepped out with my two roommates to experience West Hollywood's version of Mardi Gras and to usher in the month of November.

November is a terrific month in Southern California. We don't have true seasons, but the weather changes from one long summer into a slightly less hot, slightly more civilized fall. Men trade tank tops for shirts with sleeves, and long pants appear. The leaves don't change, but the clothing does.

Mid month, I was reminded of the several unanswered letters in my desk drawer by the arrival of another, this one from Mary Lee. As I carried the letter to my bedroom—I had begun to expect bad news and preferred it in private—I remembered a story she had told me while rehearsing one of our many Sunday performances.

Mary Lee worked as a beautician. Her dual role as beautician and pastor's wife meant she was often called on to do the hair and makeup of recently deceased parishioners. Accustomed to engaging her live clients in long and involved conversations, Mary Lee carried on extended, though one-sided, talks with her dead subjects as well, often spilling gossipy tidbits too scandalous to be repeated at the salon. After admitting this to me, Mary Lee would giggle and repeat the old adage, "Dead men tell no tales."

Once at the local funeral home, Mary Lee was working on a woman's makeup and talking up a storm about the misfortunes of some poor, unfortunate wretch when suddenly a corpse on another table sat bolt upright. Ap-

parently the man's nerves and muscles had not been sev-
ered, and the body had an involuntary, somewhat common reaction. But Mary Lee didn't bother sticking
around for the scientific explanation. She bolted from the
building like a blue streak and then worried her dead-
man-only gossip might be repeated.

Mary Lee stated in her short letter that she could not believe I had chosen to "live life so contrary to what God says
can be for someone He has created." She questioned my
salvation, bringing up a conversation we'd had more than
ten years earlier.

I was 16 at the time. My family had just moved to
Indiana and had trekked back to Tennessee for a weekend
visit. A group from Believers' Chapel went out for pizza,
and I'd asked my parents if afterward I could spend the
night with Ken and Mary Lee since I didn't get to see them
often. Actually, I just wanted to spend time with someone
other than my puritanical parents.

My parents consented, and Ken, Mary Lee, and I had
lounged and discussed my life in Indiana. Ken turned the conversation to spiritual matters. I explained that I was still involved with church but not as much as I'd been in Tennessee.
I also said I didn't agree with the strict rules my father placed
on me and that I wanted to be a regular teenager and enjoy life
like the kids at my new school. I voiced the opinion that all my
father wanted was for me to read the Bible and pray.

Ken listened quietly, then asked, "Are you a Christian?"

"I am," I answered. And then I spewed forth a tirade wondering why I couldn't be a Christian and still enjoy myself. After several minutes I calmed down, caught my breath, and asked the question that had been bothering me all along, "Why do fundamentalist Christians feel the need to be separate from everyone else?"

Ken and Mary Lee, instead of answering, interpreted my query as an indication that I hadn't been properly "saved." They immediately launched into frenetic prayer, urging me to invite Jesus into my heart. This continued for 20 or 30 minutes, though it felt like hours. Eventually I realized that if Ken and Mary Lee didn't hear a prayer from me they might never let up. I remember thinking I should have stayed with my parents. At least my father's admonitions ended at bedtime. So I prayed. I prayed aloud for Jesus to enter my heart, even though I knew he was already there. Ken and Mary Lee accompanied my halfhearted efforts with a wailing chorus of "Amens!" and "Praise the Lords!"

I fell asleep that night feeling betrayed. Ken and Mary Lee had not understood me, had not listened to me. My message that I loved God but needed to figure out how spirituality fit into my life did not sink in. I never said I'd turned my back on God, only that I'd lost faith in the Believers' Chapel interpretation of Christianity.

In her letter Mary Lee turned this ten-year-old misinter-pretation into the basis of my homosexuality, writing that when I turned my back on God, I "opened [myself] up to strong holds from the enemy, and it is a downhill slide."

I decided to write Mary Lee and attempt to explain my spirituality, my love of God, and the love I still felt for her.

November 16, 1992

Dear Mary Lee,

Thank you for your letter. I felt love from you, and that means a great deal. I love you as well. Please tell Ken I am sorry I have not returned his letter. Feel free to share this with him if you like.

While I really don't want to go into a long discourse of my homosexuality, I do want you to know that spiritu-ally I have never been more at peace. I am much closer to God now that I am not denying my homosexuality. When I was trying to live as a heterosexual, I was lying to myself, my family, and my friends, and this kept me from God. I was not rejoicing in the beautiful creation that he made.

Mary Lee, I do love God, and Christ lives within me. I am on a spiritual path now that is comfortable for me and that allows me to commune with God daily. I have not been placed on this earth to judge you or your lifestyle choices, and I pray that you will not judge me either. I want to love and be loved, that is all.

Thank you again for your caring note and for all the love and support you give Mom and Dad. I love them dearly.

Love,

Stuart

This letter I mailed, happy to respond without justifying my choices, my life, or my spirituality. I merely stated facts and asked Mary Lee, and through her, Ken, to love me and not judge me. This newly found self-assuredness, I hoped, would carry me through what I already knew would be the biggest test of my fragile independence—the upcoming holidays, Thanksgiving and Christmas.

CHAPTER 5

THE HOLIDAY OFFENSIVE

Norman Rockwell meets Tennessee Williams. That's how I thought of the Howell-Miller holidays. On the surface our gatherings were an American fantasy, overflowing with family, food, games, and laughter. But underneath lurked a subtext of unspoken drama. It might be the marriage of an aunt and uncle hanging by a thread, the grandmother who drank bourbon mixed with Valium from morning to night, the grandchild who flunked out of yet another school, or the aunt who committed suicide rather than face divorce. Unspoken secrets are what I remember most—juicy turkeys, sweet hams, joy, and the unwritten family law: Shut up, or you'll spoil the holiday.

I had broken the law. I had spilled the beans and been banished. In the Howell-Miller clan, secrets are as sacred as Jesus.

No memory of this is more vivid than the summer when I was 11. It was a beautiful, hot afternoon, and my brother and I were in the backyard playing. My father called us inside and told us to join him and Mother in their bedroom. Monty and I huddled on the way; either someone had died, or we were in for the scolding of our lives. The last time we had been called into their bedroom was to learn that my mother was pregnant with Amy. This was serious.

They sat on the edges of their swing-out twin beds. Monty and I sat at their feet. My father stiffly informed us that Mother had something to tell us. I could sense her uneasiness. She spoke in a bitter voice.

"I was married once, before I met your father," she said. "I was very young, and the marriage lasted less than a year. I didn't want to tell you, but your great-grandmother is getting senile, and she told your cousins a few months ago. I felt that it was better for you to hear it from me than from them."

I was spinning. My mother, a divorced woman. That meant she was not a virgin when she married my father. And wait, maybe he wasn't my father. Maybe I was the product of this short-lived marriage. That would explain everything. My brother is three years older than I am, and it was impossible for my mother to have had both of us in a marriage that lasted less than a year, but that didn't stop me from wishing. Or asking.

"No," Mother answered, annoyed at my obvious enjoyment of her scandalous past. "I had no children during this marriage. I wanted to wait and tell you when you were older and were possibly going to make the same mistake that I made, but I've told you now. And I never want to talk about it again."

That was it. The meeting had lasted less than five minutes but forever changed the way I viewed my family. I wondered what other cracks were hidden in our mirror of perfection. I felt closer to my mother, knowing we both had secrets. The only difference was hers had been unearthed while mine stayed buried.

Years later, as an adult, I again broached the subject with my mother. I wanted to know more about the man who could have been my father if the marriage had lasted. What was he like? Did she still know him? I had pictured him in my head as a creative genius, an actor or painter whose tortured life would have been brightened if only my mother had stayed with him. He was the loving father I longed for, the man that would have nurtured my artistic bent and accepted my differences.

"I wouldn't know him if he walked up and slapped me in the face," Mother said. "It's over and done with. I don't want to talk about it."

Southern families hide their skeletons. Forever. As far as I know, no one else has ever mentioned my mother's first marriage.

With Thanksgiving less than a week away, my mind fixed on the Norman Rockwell rather than Tennessee Williams memories of our gatherings, on the fun I'd be missing now that I was no longer welcome at my family's Thanksgiving table.

By noon, an assortment of relatives and hangers-on would arrive at Aunt Brenda and Uncle Ray's large log cabin. The men would gather in the den to watch football. The women would congregate in the kitchen to cook and gossip. During my teens I'd forced myself to join the men, but after a few years gave up the pretense of enjoying the ball games and manly chatter. My place was in the kitchen, where Aunt Brenda and I would share a predinner drink, to the chagrin of my mother. At 1 o'clock the family would assemble in the dining room for the requisite pre-buffet prayer. Everyone would nervously eye the food, hoping my father would limit himself to a few words, but steeling themselves for a sermon. We would come alive on "In Jesus' name, Amen," and stuff ourselves beyond repair. In the evening we would eat leftovers, then hunker down for a late-night game of Rook. Very Norman Rockwell.

My California roommates' plans for an authentic downhome Thanksgiving only emphasized that this would be my first holiday not spent with the Howell-Miller family. Scott planned the menu, assigning both John and me a dish. I made my mother's famous twice-baked potatoes. John cooked the ham. Scott prepared the vegetables, stuffing, and dessert. Our tiny kitchen filled with aromas that reminded me of home.

In true Miller-Howell fashion, I ignored the Tennessee Williams script I was living and painted on a brave, smiling Norman Rockwell face. But inside I was a basket case, imagining my aunts, uncles, cousins, siblings, and parents gathered without me. The worst part was that I was not sure if anyone beyond the immediate family and my aunt and uncle knew the reason I wasn't there. I imagined my mother gritting her teeth, telling my grandparents I was too busy with work to make it. What a lie. I would have jumped on a plane and flown all night to be there. Instead, I was exiled for telling the truth.

My roommates had each spent many holidays away from home. It occurred to me as we sat down to dinner that our feast had been prepared primarily for my benefit. John beamed as he sliced the ham. Scott raved about my potatoes. I nearly ruined dessert by drooling on it. I wanted our meal to last forever, but by 3 o'clock we were finished. My stomach was full, but my heart was empty. I traveled in my mind to my aunt's kitchen, the annual Rook tournament, and the family I loved.

I spent the next few weeks preparing for Christmas. I had always been the best gift buyer in the family, shopping for weeks to find the perfect present for each family member. I shoved aside my memories of Thanksgiving and the preceding few months and shopped as usual. I bought fashionable but conser-

vative clothes for my sisters and nephew and similarly thought-
ful gifts for the rest of the family. I mailed the gifts early, hoping they might trigger a change of heart and an invitation home.

They didn't.

The month passed quickly, and Christmas arrived before
I knew it. My friend Bel, a 48 year-old divorced mother of
two in her second year of graduate work at Vanderbilt's
Theology School, had decided to fly in from Tennessee to
spend the holiday with me. I was excited about her visit.
Her Bible-belt involvement with AIDS patients at
Nashville Cares had opened her eyes to the odiousness of
religion-fueled bigotry, and she had become an avid sup-
porter of gay rights, as well as a much-needed mother figure to many of our clients. I had told her about the rift with
my parents and, though she was shocked, she encouraged
me to keep the faith. "God will work it out," she had said.

I picked her up at the airport a few days before Christmas, desperately needing her spunk to lift my sagging
spirits. I almost didn't recognize her when she came down
the ramp. She had dyed and permed her hair. I kidded that
she looked like a '70s Barbra Streisand, but she didn't appreciate the joke. On the drive home I detoured through
Beverly Hills and Bel Air. She feigned interest but was
more concerned with me than the denizens of 90210. I, on
the other hand, needed the comfort of superficiality. She
allowed it, and I held my tenuous grip on sanity.

Scott greeted us at the door and gave Bel a big hug. Bel and Scott had become friends when he and I were dating, and he always thought she was special. John had flown back to Tennessee to spend the holiday with his family, so Bel's presence filled an empty space in Scott's heart as well as mine.

We spent our first night together reminiscing and chatting. Bel filled us in on the latest gossip. Scott and I regaled her with "star" sightings and Hollywood glamour. We decided to spend Christmas Eve with friends, and Christmas day driving up the coast—a trip Bel and I had been planning since my move to Los Angeles.

I knew reconciliation with my family was not imminent but hoped the Christmas season would soften my parents' position. I dreamed of a call or letter inviting me home for the holidays. I even compiled a list of available flights so that Bel and I could make a last-minute dash to Tennessee if the opportunity arose.

My parents didn't write or call, but I received a letter from my Uncle Jerry's girlfriend, Linda. She had dated Jerry, my mother's brother, in high school and was a good friend of my mother's when they were teens. She and Jerry grew apart and married other people, but after Jerry's wife died and Linda divorced her husband, they began seeing each other again.

Linda had been fighting cancer for several years and seemed to have found inner peace. Shortly before I moved to Los Angeles, my mother and I had taken her to lunch when she was in Nashville receiving chemotherapy. Even in her weakened state, she was a joy to be around. Linda talked about her son and daughters and my Uncle Jerry, astounding my mother and me with her strong will to live and her lack of concern for her own pain. She was far more interested in the happiness of those around her.

Her letter was the first positive response I'd received from my family. She wrote that she had heard about my parents' reaction to my news and that it dismayed her. I could count on her to be my friend, she said. She invited me to call or visit anytime. Her closing was simple and direct: "If you don't get home for the holidays, I'll be thinking of you. Hang in there, babe! Much love, Linda."

Her note was easily the best Christmas present I received that year. I ran to the telephone and dialed as quickly as I could. Without my years of piano training, my nervous fingers would never have completed the task. We talked for almost an hour, and I felt as if I had connected with an angel. She encouraged me to keep the faith and not give up on my family. "Those Howells are stubborn, but they're good people," she said. "I know that your mom will come around."

After my conversation with Linda, I was happy and ready to celebrate Christmas with Bel and Scott, pausing only to write a short letter before we left for dinner.

Dear Linda,

I cannot thank you enough for the card and conversation. If there was ever a Christmas angel, you qualify. This has been a very difficult time, and yours were the first kind words I've heard from my family—and yes, you are my family. I was just talking with friends and kept calling you my Aunt Linda!

I am so glad that God has placed you in our lives and am especially thankful that you have given Uncle Jerry so much happiness. His life has not always been an easy one, and he deserves someone like you. Your nonjudgmental attitude has had an effect on him and may on the rest of our family too.

Thank you for your love and support. I will keep in touch and hope that you have a wonderful Christmas and New Year.

Peace and love,

Stuart

On Christmas Eve day I heard from my family. I answered a knock at the door, expecting to find a neighbor dressed in drag as Mrs. Claus. Instead it was Federal Express with a package from home. Bel and Scott watched as I tore open the box. Inside were homemade candies and a note from my mother.

She thanked me for the Christmas gifts but said they weren't necessary, that all my family wanted was for me to "repent" my sin of homosexuality. She told me how they planned to spend Christmas day, then wrote, "It would be better if you don't contact Monty for a while. He is having trouble with high blood pressure and doesn't need any stress at this time."

I handed the note to Bel. I couldn't cry. I couldn't speak. I couldn't feel. My hopes for a speedy reconciliation were absurd. My father, and by extension my family, would never give up. Bel placed a hand on my shoulder. "It will be OK," she said. "I'm here, and I love you."

Bel had chosen to spend Christmas with me instead of her own family. She had chosen me as her holiday companion. It was time for me to return her love. Her words pulled me through the rest of the day and Christmas Eve dinner at my friends' house. But even a raucous dinner party couldn't hold my attention. I kept thinking about my mother's note and the fact that I was in Los Angeles instead of Tennessee.

I awoke Christmas morning with mixed emotions—excitement, sadness, joy, despair. In the bathroom I stared at myself in the mirror. I looked the same as always. My parents acted as if I'd grown horns, hooves, and a tail. One simple declarative sentence—I am gay—had ended a lifetime of love. Bel knocked at the door, breaking my reverie. "Are you about finished in there?" she asked in her beautiful Southern voice. "Yes," I answered. "I'll be right there."

Our weekend jaunt was just what I needed. The beauty of the California coast took my breath away. Every time we thought we had just seen the most magnificent view in the world, we'd round a bend and see something even more beautiful. This was Bel's first Christmas away from her family too. She wanted and needed to create her own life after her divorce and was as happy to be with me as I was with her. Still, it was a difficult time for both of us. We spent three days immersed in nature's beauty, talking little but taking comfort in each other.

Bel went to bed early our first night back in Los Angeles. I sat on the balcony, composed my thoughts, and wrote a letter to my mother.

December 28, 1992

Dear Mother,

I am hurting very much. My heart feels as if it will break. So many thoughts are going on that I'm not really sure where to start. I guess I should start by saying how much I love you. I love you so much, and I am so angry and hurt that you continue to treat me so horribly. If you wanted to drive a stake through my heart and cause me tremendous pain, you succeeded. I could not believe the letter you sent me on Christmas Eve, the day before Christ's birth, a day that should signify love and healing. I feel your letter was hateful and manipulative. Why didn't you just burn my gifts if you felt this way?

How could you tell me not to contact my own brother? And then to say you are interested in my life—Is this so you won't feel guilty when people ask about me? Why don't you start being honest. If you hate me or have anger, why won't you just say it? I have no desire to talk to you about the weather or my job. I want to talk, really talk, about what is going on. I wanted to call you Christmas morning but feared you would reject me again. And you are rejecting me. Please don't try to convince yourself that you are rejecting the sin and not the sinner because I don't buy that and don't think you do either. I am your son, your flesh and blood. How can you continue this?

You said to me in August that you had always taken up for me and felt like I had stabbed you in the back. Well, that's a two-way street. I feel like you are the one who has stabbed me and rejected me. Are you scared to love me as I really am? Do you think retreating to the Bible allows you to justify all of this? Do you think it will bring happiness and wholeness to our family? I haven't seen that approach work in 27 years. I wish you could see the reality of our family and not the picture you seem to have painted. I believe that love, real love, can heal our relationship, and only God can show us how to do that. Have you felt God's love in your life since August? Was God's love in the letter you wrote me?

Mother, I have to tell you that I don't want to hear from you or dad again until you are ready to talk and listen. I am not going to change, nor do I want to. Does that mean I'm different from the son you gave birth to, the son you raised, the son you love? No! It means I am living the life that makes me happy, the life that is mine, not yours.

You can choose to be a part of that life or not. By choosing no, you will be missing out on a son who loves you, loves others, loves himself, and most importantly loves God. Choosing to be a part of my life does not mean making my choices for me or agreeing with them, anymore than I can make or agree with yours. It means loving me, not judging me. It means allowing me to be me, which I believe is the greatest gift anyone can ever give another person.

I will not choose a life of pain simply because you are upset. If you need to work through this, do it, but quit hurting me in the process.

I will always love you,

Stuart

I placed the letter aside and crawled into bed. As I drifted off, I decided to not send the letter. My words were too cruel. They were not intended to heal, but to wound. I wanted my mother to hurt as much as I did. But too much pain had already passed between us. I prayed that the new year would bring hope and healing. I said good-bye to 1992 and hello to a new year—and a new onslaught of prayer warriors.

CHAPTER 6

BOMBS AWAY

I dropped Bel at the airport amid the hustle and bustle of holiday travelers returning home and breathed a sigh of relief. Thanks to the support of friends—and Marianne Williamson—I had survived the season. The sky hadn't fallen, the world hadn't stopped spinning, and we hadn't even had an earthquake. I drove home vowing that the new year marked a new chapter in my life. No more feeling sorry for myself. No, sir, I was on the road to recovery.

I just didn't realize the road would be so bumpy.

When I arrived home I spotted a stack of mail on the kitchen counter. To my delight, the only letter was from my sister-in-law, Barbara. I had not heard from her or Monty over the holidays and had begun to worry they had joined the prayer warriors.

Her letter was a mixed bag—newsy, chatty, loving, and preachy. She told me that Monty had indeed been troubled by high blood pressure and was taking medication. He'd had a few "mini-blackout spells," but tests revealed no serious disorders. She went on to say she didn't agree with my lifestyle and knew in her heart that I was sinning. She told me I couldn't continue without experiencing God's wrath. "As a Christian, you can't lose your salvation, but you can die a physical death, a premature death." She questioned whether I was happy, then said, "I'm not condemning you, but I can't accept your lifestyle as glorifying God."

The prayer warriors had gotten to her; there was no other explanation for her change of heart. I couldn't blame her, though. After all, she still lived in Murfreesboro and communed daily with my family and her family—Believers' Chapel parishioners.

She closed by telling me there were ministries for homosexuals, including several in Los Angeles. She offered to send me the addresses if I wanted them. She also told me she was sending a book for me to read. I couldn't wait.

I put the letter down and retreated to my bedroom where I opened the bottom drawer of my dresser, reached into the farthest corner, and pulled a single beautiful white cigarette from a pack I'd hidden under a tattered pair of ski socks. I stepped outside, onto the balcony, and looked around to make sure no one was watching. Then I lit up. I had quit smoking six months before, but the stress of the holidays had sent me, ever so secretly, back into the arms of my soothing friend. Maybe the prayer warriors were right. Maybe God *was* killing me. Slowly. Through cigarettes.

I blew smoke rings and thought about Barbara's letter. It was every bit as judgmental as the rest, but at least she was willing to discuss things in a rational manner. That was more than I could say for my mother, father, or aunt. But it still depressed me, and all I wanted to do was sleep. I was tired of justifying my "lifestyle choice." What a lifestyle! Have a difficult childhood, lose your family, and get bashed by religious homophobes. Want to sign up?

I folded the letter and placed it and the others I'd received in the bottom drawer of my dresser, right next to my cigarettes. I figured that if I had to see the stack of letters every time I wanted a cigarette, I wouldn't smoke. It didn't work, but it was a good idea.

The next day I returned to work, happy to be back in the collective bosom of my Gay and Lesbian Center family. The office buzzed with holiday stories—outrageous gifts, travel nightmares, pounds gained. I told a few people about driving up the coast with Bel, but my tale sounded sad, and I quit repeating it.

In the afternoon my boss, Julia, knocked on my door. "Can I come in for a minute?" she asked, entering and closing the door without waiting for an answer, not that I would have said no. "How are you *really* doing?" she asked.

Julia was the reason I moved to California. I had met her a year earlier when I helped John move from Tennessee to Los Angeles. She was director of education and was looking for a new project director. A mutual friend who had previously held the position suggested that since I was in town, I should interview. I met with Julia and felt as if I'd known her forever. We talked for more than an hour, and by the end of the meeting she had offered me the job. I told her I would think about it and would let her know.

By the time I returned to Nashville I had cold feet. It was a great opportunity, but there was no way I could uproot myself and move across the country. What if it didn't work out? In Tennessee I had resources, a boyfriend, and family. In Los Angeles I had one friend, John. I reluctantly declined her offer.

Four months later the phone rang. Julia. "It's been four months, and we still can't find the right person," she said. "I keep coming back to you, and I wondered if maybe you might change your mind." I thought about it for a few seconds and suddenly heard myself saying yes. I wasn't sure why they wanted a country boy from Tennessee, but I wasn't going to fight it anymore. The job had remained open for four months, waiting for me to take it. It was meant to be. And besides, my boyfriend and I had broken up, and I needed a change.

Julia had become one of my closest friends, and I couldn't lie to her. I spilled my guts, telling her I felt as if my foundation had slipped out from under me, that I didn't know who I was outside the context of family, and that I didn't know if I would be able to continue if no one cared about me.

Julia shocked me with her response. "Stuart, sometimes families suck." She laughed when my jaw dropped. Usually, her counseling took a more serious tone. "All I can tell you," she said, "is that you are going to do great things in your life. Everyone here loves you, and you're going to get through this."

I realized that people did care about me. I instantly felt better and got on with my day. If only my day hadn't involved a trip to the mailbox.

The letter was long, tedious, repetitive, and it was written in faux Biblical style. "Keep your eyes on Jesus," it ordered. "Think about His patience as sinful men did horrible things to Him." The letter told me that God had said, "My son, don't be angry when the Lord punishes you. Don't be discouraged when He has to show you where you are wrong. For when He punishes you, it proves that He loves you. When He whips you, it proves you are really His child." The letter admonished me to "stand firm and follow a straight path," to "seek to live a clean and holy life," to "obey Him who is speaking to you." I was told to prepare for "terror, flaming fire, gloom, darkness, and a terrible storm.... For our God is a consuming fire." The letter was signed, "Joe and Joyce."

I wondered: Who in the world are Joe and Joyce? And where did they get my address?

I checked the envelope. The return address said Florida. Florida? The prayer warriors had gone national. I fumed as I pictured my mother and father giving my address to total strangers. I imagined my photo plastered on milk cartons and church bulletin boards throughout the South. "Lost: Stuart Miller. Last seen in the arms of the devil." I tossed the letter to John and lit up.

"What the hell are you doing?" he asked. He hadn't caught me smoking yet.

"Oh, just shut up and read," I replied.

He made it through the first few paragraphs before throwing the letter aside. "This is getting a little scary," he said.

"You want scary?" I said. "Here's scary. I have no idea who these people are."

I was enraged. I didn't mind people knowing I was gay, but I couldn't stomach hateful letters from people I'd never met.

A second letter from Joe and Joyce arrived a few days later. "You are a handsome young man with a winning smile," it began. So they *had* met me. A glutton for flattery, I read on, only to be disappointed. They had nothing else nice to say, telling me that God had given me the "the perfect parents." They knew who I was but had clearly confused my mother and father with some other couple.

I added the letter to the growing stack in my drawer.

The next week was mercifully quiet. Work chugged busily along. We planned a major outreach effort and a fund-raiser, but my mind was elsewhere. I had lost my equilibrium, and no one really understood my situation. None of my friends were from a fundamentalist background. Their reactions ranged from shock, to disbelief, to sympathy. But not empathy. I had known coming out carried consequences. I had experienced the tight grip of fundamentalism many times over. But none of my friends understood that being a Christian fundamentalist meant giving up your heart, mind, and emotions to blindly follow the words of the Bible. Even a mother's love came second to the word of God.

In some ways, fundamentalist Christianity was an easy life. Self-esteem was not relevant. Struggle and self-exploration were pointless. All I had to do was read and pray. Depression, anxiety, sorrow, and pain were manifestations of the fall of man and would disappear if I believed and prayed hard enough. "Just put your eyes on the Cross," my father told me, "and everything will be taken care of." Life was easy because I had no input.

Within days I received yet another letter from Joe and Joyce, as well as a note from my Cousin Jan. I decided to read the strangers' first since Jan's, coming from a family member, was potentially more hurtful.

Joe and Joyce wrote about their daughter. She had gotten involved with the wrong man, and it had taken four years of prayer to help her see she'd made a mistake. "We reap what we sow," they said.

I hoped that would be true for this meddling duo. Mention of their daughter, however, rang a bell. Finally, I knew who these people were—and it had only taken three letters.

When I was away at college, my parents told me about a young woman who had been in a terrible car accident. Her parents lived in another state, so my mother and father kindly opened their guest house to the couple so that they could be near their hospitalized daughter. I met Joe and Joyce briefly on a visit home. They shared the same religious views as my parents. My father scored big by enlisting them in his prayer brigade. They were tenacious warriors.

I opened Jan's letter. She cut to the chase, telling me she didn't know until after the holidays that I had told the family I was gay. "I want you to know," she wrote, "that even though I would have wished a different lifestyle for you, it is your life, and you have to do and be what is right for you. I know that not everyone in the family has been supportive, and I'm sorry about that." She went on to say she would always be there for me and that if I ever needed her, all I had to do was ask. "You are always welcome in my home," she wrote. She signed off by telling me I had always been, and would always be, her favorite cousin.

I wept. Her words meant more to me than I will ever be able to express. They were also unexpected, as Jan and I had not spoken much over the past several years. We had been close growing up, but that closeness did not extend into adulthood. Our paths had taken us in different directions. I attended college, enjoying a life of fraternity parties and spring breaks. She married and in quick succession had two children. The only time we'd seen each other over the past five or six years had been for a few hours at Christmas.

I remembered the fun we'd had as children. Jan was three years older and lived on my grandfather's farm, where her father worked as manager. When my family visited I enjoyed riding horses and playing outside with Monty and Jan's brothers, Jeff and Jake, but had much more fun in Jan's lace-filled bedroom playing with Barbies and baking sweets in her Easy-Bake Oven. Sometimes Jake would join us in a game of Dream Date. Jan, along with her brothers and her mother, Jeanette, never questioned my enjoyment of "girl" games. Their home was one of the few places where I felt comfortable and loved for who I was.

Then when I was in college, Aunt Jeanette committed suicide. The entire family was devastated. There had been no warning signs. Or perhaps, as denial runs rampant in our family, the signs had been ignored. Even though she and Uncle Jerry were divorcing after many rocky years of marriage, her life seemed to be going well. She had enrolled in nursing school and seemed excited about the prospect of moving into the city and starting over. She had never been happy with farm life, and everyone believed the breakup was the best thing for her and my uncle.

The funeral was difficult, full of tension and emotion. I didn't know how to comfort my cousins. We had spent our childhood sharing everything and suddenly were separated by miles of grief and pain. Not surprisingly, we suffered in silence. We never discussed Jeanette's death after the funeral.

I grieved for my aunt once again, knowing I could never thank her for the unconditional love and support she had given me as a child. She had sat and listened to me play the piano in her living room, encouraging my talent and building my nonexistent self-esteem. Even in my teenage years, she took an interest in me. We would sit for hours and talk about her latest redecorating idea or my high school activities. I was sure she would have accepted my homosexuality and loved me no matter what, as her daughter had.

I phoned Jan to thank her for her letter. I heard her sons vying for attention in the background. "Sh-h-h, Mama's on the phone," she said. She told me my grandparents had not been told the reason for my absence over the holidays. We also talked about her mother. I told her how much I had loved and now missed her mother. She told me how alone she felt, that no one had ever discussed the suicide with her. As we talked the years disappeared. We were back in her bedroom sharing our secrets, our joys, and our sorrows. We were connected again. It felt wonderful to have Jan back in my life. I only wished we hadn't waited so long to reach out.

That night I replayed Jan's words in my mind. I began to understand that God wouldn't give me more than I could handle. Whenever I thought things were hopeless, a sign would appear that reassured me of the love that existed in the world. Jan's letter was one of those signs. She was still the only blood relative to offer love rather than judgment, but it was a start. Just knowing there was one person who had loved me my entire life, warts and all, helped me believe I would survive my ordeal.

A week passed with no letters from the prayer brigade. And then I was hit with a succession of bombs. The first was a plain white postcard from my father that contained only the date, his signature, and a typewritten Bible verse:

"For the time will come when they will not endure sound doctrine; but wanting to have their ears tickled, they will accumulate for themselves teachers in accordance to their own desires; and will turn aside to myths. (2 Timothy 4:3-4)." An attached sticker read, "Love never gives up. (1 Corinthians 13:7)."

The following day I received a letter from a couple in my parent's church. They had two daughters around the age of my brother and me, and we had grown up doing church activities together. I think my brother even dated one of the girls. They were a sweet, simple family and had always been kind to me. I'm sure the couple identified with my parents' dilemma, as their oldest daughter, Sarah, had been a rebellious teen. As the letters went, this was one of the least offensive. They said they were thinking of me even though I had chosen "to follow the wrong spirit." I filed their letter with the others and thanked God that neither my father's postcard nor this letter troubled me too much. I felt at peace and knew my broken spirit was healing. I was prepared to move on, to leave my church and family behind and seek a more accepting love and spirituality. I would fight no more. For me, the prayer war was over.

Then I received a letter from Joyce, of Joe and Joyce. She had little to say—nothing new, anyway—but enclosed a photocopy of an eight page letter written by a woman named Darlene to her teenage nephew, Robert, who had told his mother he was gay.

Darlene confessed to her nephew that she had been a lesbian for many years. "It's lonely," she wrote. "It's hard. It's not God's plan. It's a lie. It's lonely because my gay friends were out for self-gratification, and I was the object toward that end." Darlene wove a tale of drugs and alcohol and unfulfilling relationships. She said, "Members of the gay community exploited me physically to satisfy their desires, but they told me they were fighting for my sexual freedom." She described homosexuality as an "unending cycle of bondage" that keeps repeating itself through recruitment of young people like Robert, who are encouraged to explore "every sexual curiosity." She warned her nephew that "male prostitution and venereal disease could become as much a part of your life as reading the daily newspaper." She wrote about the "abomination," then extolled the virtues of "natural" roles for men and women. "What your gay friends will never tell you," she said, "is that being gay isn't a right—it's a sin."

I put the letter down. I was not the only victim of a prayer war. There was Robert, and perhaps others—less connected, less able to care for themselves, less able to fight. The initial letters had hurt me. This one pissed me off. I decided to stop feeling sorry for myself and to start working to help people like Robert. I decided to fight.

I told Scott my news over dinner. "Doesn't she know that the reason so many kids commit suicide isn't that they're gay," I said, "but because of hateful lunatics like her who convince them there's something wrong with them, something evil and unnatural. I have to fight back."

After dinner I went to a friend's house to watch a movie. Distracted, all I could think about was Robert. Had he found his way out of that homophobic environment, or had his aunt's letter pushed him over the edge into suicide or an unhappy life filled with lies and deceit? And what about Darlene? Gay life can be difficult, but so can straight life. She clearly did not recognize that her letter described the symptoms of societally sanctioned homophobia rather than an inherent flaw in homosexuals. Her misery was her own. Not mine. Not Robert's.

I vowed to find a way to make a difference for people like Robert, and even Darlene. My pain and sadness transformed into strength. I would conquer my fear of loss and rejection. If my father wanted to fight a war for my soul, I would give him a war. But I would battle for more souls than just mine.

CHAPTER 7

NOT EXACTLY QUIET
ON THE WESTERN FRONT

February was warm and sunny and matched my disposition. I felt as if I had emerged from the eye of a storm and was now comfortably resting in the disheveled, happy heap I called my life. The clouds had lifted. I was becoming my old Pollyanna self again. And I hadn't even needed Prozac.

At work we busily prepared for Stop AIDS week, an annual outreach campaign culminating in a fashion show and ceremony honoring community role models. This was the first major fund-raiser I had coordinated in Los Angeles and, needless to say, I wanted everything to be perfect. I wanted people to know that a Tennessee boy could throw an L.A. party with style and flair.

At the same time, others at work prepared for the march on Washington, which I planned to attend. In fact, I could hardly wait to go. I planned a vacation around the event, including a week in Boston to visit my best friend from high school in Indiana, Scott, a different Scott from my present roommate.

Scott was the smartest student in our class—athletic, funny, and involved in many school activities, including the student council and drama club. In Indiana we had been inseparable, and I had secretly had a crush on him. I didn't find out until years later that he was gay. We lost touch after high school, and I hadn't heard from him until I moved to California. Then, in a subtly worded letter, he let the cat out of the bag, saying he had gone through a few "lifestyle adjustments." We easily reconnected as though we had never been apart. I was excited to see him again after so many years apart.

I also planned to visit Larry, whom I'd met in Washington, D.C., at the AIDS conference I'd attended before coming out to my parents. Our steamy weeklong affair had fizzled when he visited me in Los Angeles a few weeks later, at the same time as Margaret, but after months of phone calls and letter writing, we decided our problems centered on my family's reaction to my homosexuality. In our letters and conversations, we had each professed our undying love for the other, and I was ready to take the plunge and marry Larry. We just had to decide who was moving. I didn't want to leave Los Angeles anymore than Larry wanted to leave Washington, but I was willing to talk about it if that was the only option.

Before I could enjoy my April vacation with Larry and Scott, though, I had to make it through February and March.

Two of my parents' neighbors, Troy and Bessie, sent letters that arrived on the same day. Bessie said she hated to see my mother and father so upset over my lifestyle. "We are all praying…that you will change and marry a pretty girl and have a wonderful family like your folks' and ours." Troy retold the tale of how an electric fence nearly killed my sister when she was a child and then said, "The lifestyle you have chosen is more dangerous than death by electric shocking. God loves you Stuart. Please do not spit in his face with this homosexual lifestyle you have chosen for yourself."

I immediately ran outside and searched for a pretty girl to marry, but the closest I could find in West Hollywood was a drunken, gravel-voiced drag queen. "I don't want to marry," she said. "I like my freedom."

Troy and Bessie were older than my parents. Their children were adults when my brother and I were still in grade school. The youngest of their two daughters, Karen, married the son of our elderly evangelical preacher at Grace Baptist. Karen and her new husband, Danny, spent the first few years of their marriage in a mother-in-law apartment Troy had built for them. As children, my sister-in-law Barbara and I loved spending time with them. They and other young couples in the church took us on camping trips, to ball games, and other fun places. Barbara and I never thought about being in the way, but I'm sure the newlyweds must have tired of our constant intrusions. They never complained, though, and we never stopped pestering them—until Grace Baptist broke apart. After that, we didn't see them as often.

Troy and Bessie were wonderful neighbors. Troy was a rugged outdoorsman who was always willing to pitch in when needed. I remember that he mowed our fields before my father bought his own tractor. Bessie worked as a grammar school cafeteria manager and had one of the sweetest dispositions of anyone I knew. If Mom had extra vegetables or blackberries, she would send me to Troy and Bessie's to share. Bessie always returned the favor, sending me back with homemade bread or preserves. It saddened me that Troy and Bessie had joined the prayer brigade.

I wanted to cry as I imagined them writing the letters they promised my parents they would send. I wanted to tell them that I was still the same little boy who brought over blackberries and went for walks in the woods with them. I was still sweet and kind and loving. I still loved their down-home ways and wanted them in my life. I still wanted them to love me. But I was uncertain how I could overcome their prejudice and fear. They had probably never known an openly gay person in their life until me, and like my sister, they could only view me through a lens distorted by the church.

A few days later, Another letter arrived from Barbara. She told me that Monty was fine. His problems were caused by high blood pressure, which could be controlled with medication, nothing more serious than that. The remainder of her letter was wishy-washy—half-supportive, half-preachy. She did say she loved me, and there was a slight hint that she might be willing to consider the possibility that being gay was simply the way I was. "I really have mixed feelings," she said. "I have no doubt that you can live that way and say you love God and really mean it. And I know beyond a shadow of a doubt that He loves you, but I just don't understand how you can really believe it's His will for you to be gay." She asked me to write back and let her know what I thought.

I had loved Barbara for as long as I could remember but suddenly felt as if I hadn't really known her at all. As children, we spent hours playing, singing, and planning our futures. In our teens, we taught Sunday school together and started a puppet ministry. And when she decided to marry my brother, even though I felt a tinge of jealousy, I was thrilled we would be connected for the rest of our lives. Barbara had never been judgmental, even when she found out I drank, smoked, and had premarital sex with Margaret.

I wondered what had happened since the time I told her and Monty I was gay. They had been supportive that evening, but in the intervening months I had not heard a word from my brother and had only received two ambivalent letters from Barbara. Furthermore, my mother had intimated that it was my fault my brother was having medical problems. Was my announcement so shocking that Monty and Barbara were unable to tell me how they really felt? Were they so caught up in my parents' pain that they could not support me or had they simply become entangled in my father's vendetta, too close to the situation to remain objective?

I wrote Barbara a heartfelt letter expressing my disappointment in her and Monty's lack of support.

February 7, 1993

Dear Barbara,

Thanks for your letter and the picture of Justin. He's growing up so fast. I hope that all is well, and I'm glad Monty is doing better. Give him my love.

I'm not sure how to respond to your letter. I am glad you are trying to understand but still feel very judged and preached at. Even done in a nice way, it feels judgmental.

One thing that is easy to clear up is the friends vs. family issue. I certainly did not mean to intimate that my friends are any more or less important than my blood relatives. But my friends are important to me, and I consider them family. Donna, Jamie, Sue, Jeff, Bel, and others have been part of my family for years. I'm sure you also have friends you consider family. That doesn't take away from the love I have for you.

There's plenty to go around. The biggest difference between my real family and my adopted family is judgmentalism. My friends have never judged me the way my family has. Maybe it's because they don't want to control me. I'm not sure.

This judgment issue is not limited to me being gay. I have always felt judged by Mom and Dad if I didn't do things the way they perceived as right. My beliefs about many things are different than yours and theirs, but what does it matter? I don't believe the ability to point to something in the Bible makes someone right. To me, the Bible is very personal and is one path to God. I believe there are other paths too. I go to a church here that I love and also study the "Course in Miracles." These are very special because they help me get to God. They may not be your path and that's fine. I don't need to judge you or your path and can't understand why people judge mine. We grew up with a very narrow view of Christianity. There is a whole world of different beliefs out there. Whether it's Mormon, Catholic, Jewish, or whatever—everyone is worshiping God.

All I ask for, Barb, is love. We don't have to agree, but we don't have to judge each other either. Part of becoming an adult for me has been defining my own values and beliefs. I think that if you look at families, each generation must come up with its own standards, beliefs, and values. The most important thing, in my opinion, is that we support each other in love while adhering to our own personal beliefs.

I do love you and Monty and Justin. However, I'm re-sponsible for my own life and happiness, as you are for yours. I love my life and wouldn't change it for the world. I don't feel that I've chosen a difficult life. I couldn't and wouldn't be any other way.

I'm sorry if I have not always reacted in a loving way. Please know that I love my family. You have been a part of my family since we were kids, and you always will be.

Take care and please continue to pray for me.

Love,

Stuart

I dropped the letter in the mailbox before going to bed, deciding that perhaps my father's advice about sleeping on letters had kept me from communicating my true feelings. I felt guilty about my family's pain and suffering, but they didn't seem to be worried about mine. My brother had not even bothered to write or call since my trip in August. It seemed ironic that they lived in the comfort of family, yet thought their pain was greater than mine. I would be patient with them, but I was not going to be a doormat. I had fought a defensive war for six months, and now I was ready to begin an offense.

My new strategy was quickly put to the test. The following week at work, while I sat at my desk, the phone rang. Joey, our administrative assistant, answered. After a short conversation, obviously annoyed at being slighted, he told me the person on the line would not identify herself but wanted to speak with me. I picked up, expecting a client afraid of outing herself. Instead, I heard a cool voice say, "Hello, this is your mother."

I had not heard her voice in more than six months. I mumbled hello and was promptly chastised for not sending her or my father birthday cards in January. I explained that while I still loved the two of them, they were treating me poorly, and I could not in good conscience wish them unfelt tidings of happiness. I also told her how much her note at Christmas, telling me my gifts had been unnecessary, hurt me.

We spent the next 15 minutes going round and round. She asked how I could have expected any other reaction from them. I stood my ground, explaining that I had never expected them to embrace my homosexuality, only to accept it. "If you really believe this is so wrong," I said, "then put it in God's hands and let him take care of it. I just want you to stop judging me and be my mother." She said she worried about me and that at least I could send a note or card every once in a while. She explained how difficult all of this was for her but agreed to try and be less judgmental. I thanked her and promised I would write more often and not punish her with silence. After we hung up I fell back in my chair, sweaty and exhausted.

I needed to share my victory and telephoned Julie, the other project director in our department. Julie is an Audrey Hepburn look-alike who had been amazed and shocked by my family's reaction. Her own family, devout Catholics, had come to terms with her sexuality and accepted her lover, Amy, as part of the family. Julie had shared my story with her mom, who could not believe that any mother would respond as mine had.

"What's wrong?" she asked.

"Nothing," I answered. I recounted the conversation with my mother, how I'd stood my ground in the face of emotional blackmail.

Julie congratulated me on my small victory. "You just have to keep reminding yourself that you've done nothing wrong," she said.

The next few weeks flew by as Chaz, our team of staff and volunteers, and I finalized preparations for Stop AIDS week. The stress of planning a weeklong series of events took its toll, though. We worked too hard and were not having fun. My usual upbeat attitude and cheery disposition eroded into grumpiness. I wanted the event to be over so I could get on with the business of enjoying my work and personal life. On the first Friday in March, just when I'd reached my breaking point, the phone rang. Scott. "When are you coming home?" he asked. "I have something special for you." He knew how stressed I'd been.

"I'll be home at 6 o'clock, but don't expect too much. I'm exhausted," I said.

A few hours later I walked into an apartment filled with soothing music and the heavenly aroma of Scott's home cooking. He took my briefcase and handed me a beer. "Right this way," he said, and led me to my bathroom. He pointed to the tub, which was filled with steaming water and floating lilacs. "I don't want to see you for at least half an hour," he said.

I poured myself into the bath and the stress of the preceding weeks and months melted away. I closed my eyes and meditated, thankful for my wonderful friends and co-workers. I could not allow an event, no matter how stressful, to make me forget how blessed I was. As the captain of the ship, I decided, I had to set an example. Come Monday, the old, familiar Stuart would return to the office.

Dinner was delicious, and we splurged on fat-free brownies and frozen yogurt for dessert. Before going to bed, I realized I had not gone through the day's mail. I sorted through and spotted a letter from my mother.

It was a short note filled with news of my family and the weather. Not a word about my sexuality. Not a single admonition or warning about my impending spiritual or physical death. I couldn't believe it. My mother had heard and honored my request to stop judging me. I turned out the light and thanked God for this small miracle and for the many other blessings in my life.

CHAPTER 8

FORWARD MARCH

April finally arrived. Scott dropped me at the airport. "It looks like you're not alone," he said. Everywhere I looked I saw freedom rings, rainbow flags, and Louis Vuitton luggage. I was so excited about seeing Larry and participating in the largest gay and lesbian march in history that I hadn't noticed the airport was filled with fellow queers until Scott mentioned it.

I struck up a conversation with two lesbians who had attended the march in 1987. They told me stories about their 15 years of activism, including struggles with workplace discrimination and several civil disobedience arrests. Perhaps my plight was not as bad as I thought. My family had reacted horribly, but I had come out at an excellent time. Gay men and lesbians were more visible and accepted than at any time in American history. Our public ranks were growing and nothing, I believed, could stop us in our quest for equality under the law.

I felt a little sorry for the business travelers on our L.A.-to-Washington flight. They sat silent and wide-eyed amid a rowdy out and proud crowd. Mardi Gras in a flying metal tube. A sight to behold.

I found Larry in the sea of faces at Washington National Airport. I dove into his arms for a big hug and lusty kiss. Our public display of affection felt natural and good. I looked around and saw dozens of couples acting similarly. This was *our* town for the next five days, and we planned to enjoy every minute of it.

Larry worked in the HIV prevention program at Whitman Walker Clinic, and we had spent many hours discussing the challenges of our similar careers. In addition, he had flirted with fundamentalist Christianity in college; consequently, he understood the pain religion can cause gays and lesbians. We were compatible both emotionally and spiritually. Fortunately for Larry, his parents recognized he was gay when he was young. They took him to the New York City Gay Pride Festival when he was 13, not saying a word about why they were there—a subtle, beautiful expression of unconditional love. Without saying a word, they were able to tell him they loved him, no matter what. I envied the relationship he had with his parents.

We met friends of Larry's for a late afternoon drink before heading to the town house he shared with two roommates. I wanted to be alone with Larry, but meeting his friends seemed like a good beginning to our lifetime together.

DuPont Circle overflowed with gays and lesbians. The streets were packed, and we were lucky to find a parking place near the bar where his friends waited. The city was electric that day. Although West Hollywood is a large and openly gay neighborhood, I had never seen the likes of this. It was if someone waved a magic wand, and we were suddenly 90% of the population instead of 10%. *Viola!*

We sat on the patio of the bar and gawked at the scene. I was mesmerized by the differences in style. In West Hollywood the look was gym bodies and work boots. Here, everyone looked unique: preppie, punk, leather, lace, cowboy, diesel-dyke, ultrafem, and more—a spectrum of humanity unlike any I had ever seen. Between the crowds, the cocktails, and my love for Larry, I was euphoric. I savored the moment, burned it into my memory. I had never been this happy in my life, and I wanted it to last forever.

It didn't.

After we left the bar, Larry dropped me at his town house and said he would meet me there later because he had to see a friend. He was mysterious about the meeting, and I knew, deep down, that something was not right. He had been distant all day, and even a little cold. But maybe I was reading too much into it, maybe I just needed to rest after the long plane trip. I put on my best smile and told Larry to take all the time he needed. I would grab a nap and then shower for a party we planned to attend later that evening.

At the party everything seemed fine. Larry was attentive, and we both had a great time. But our lovemaking that night was passionless. The person who couldn't keep his hands off me had disappeared.

The next few days were spent shopping, sight-seeing, and preparing for that Sunday's march. Larry was busy helping Whitman Walker Clinic prepare for the event, so I spent most of my time with friends from Los Angeles and Nashville. On Saturday, Larry and I met two of my best friends from Tennessee, Chuck and Phil, for lunch. Chuck and I had once been romantically involved, and Phil was the friend I stayed with after coming out to my family. We spent the afternoon party-hopping our way through gay Washington. As we drank more and more, Chuck began to express doubts about Larry and me. I, too, was concerned, but Larry hadn't said a word, and I didn't want to seem like a nervous Nellie. Chuck and Phil encouraged me to talk to Larry to see what was going on.

As Larry and I made our way home that evening, holding hands and walking the streets of Washington, I swallowed hard and asked if everything was all right between us. I told him I wanted to spend my life with him. He stopped walking and dropped my hand. He had been seeing someone else for several months, he said, and hadn't known how to tell me. He loved me, but he loved the other person too. He didn't know what to do.

I was furious. I didn't care that he was seeing someone else, but he had not been honest with me. He had written me beautiful letters filled with talk of marriage while seeing another man. I felt like a fool. I could have handled the fact that he was in love with someone else. We could have worked through it and at least maintained our friendship. But I had struggled so painfully for truth, and he knew it, so his lying was more than I could bear.

I said a few choice words and went mute. I had nothing else to say to him. I had trusted him with my most intimate desires—not sexual desires but desires for love and family—and he had betrayed me. At least my family had been honest about their feelings. Larry had lied, offering no defense except his desire to spare my feelings.

We made it back to his apartment, and I ran upstairs and crawled into bed. I woke the next morning alone. Larry had probably spent the night with his new love, and frankly, I didn't care. I showered and dressed—Stop AIDS/Lifeguard Project T-shirt, denim shorts, tennis shoes, and parade whistle. I had planned to march with Larry and the Washington contingent but decided to find the Los Angeles group instead. I would march with my coworkers from the Gay and Lesbian Center.

Larry and his roommates were downstairs in the kitchen, talking and preparing sandwiches for the parade. They fell silent when I entered. They all knew about the argument, and they probably also knew about Larry's other boyfriend, making me angry at all of them. All I wanted to do was grab a Coke and get the hell out.

"Are you ready to go?" Larry asked, looking like a puppy who has just peed on the new living room carpet.

"I'm marching with Los Angeles," I answered.

Just then the phone rang. It was for me. Standing in the kitchen, surrounded by Larry and his roommates, I took the call, expecting someone from L.A. I had left Larry's number on my answering machine in case of an emergency and had also given it to a few friends who would be at the march.

I heard a shaky voice say, "Please don't do this to us." It was my mother, near tears.

"What are you talking about?" I asked.

She told me she knew about the march and begged me to not take part. She said it was all over the television and that my grandparents might die if they saw me. I told her that people didn't die from learning their grandchild is gay, but she wouldn't let up and kept begging me not to go. I told her she was attempting emotional blackmail and that I would not put up with it. Finally, fed up with her hysterics and aware that every eye in the room was on me, I did something I had never done. I hung up on my mother.

"I'm out of here," I said. I grabbed my fanny pack and left Larry's apartment.

I made my way to the Washington Monument, crying, searching for the Los Angeles contingent. Here I was, surrounded by hundreds of thousands of people, and more alone than ever. I wanted to click my heels and wake up in Los Angeles with Scott and John.

I found the Los Angeles contingent but waited until I had stopped crying before joining them. No one would want to hear my sob story on such a happy and monumental occasion, so I opted for a stiff upper lip and lots of lying. "Oh, no, everything's fine with Larry. I just decided I wanted to march with my L.A. family," I offered to anyone who asked. It occurred to me that I was doing exactly what I had condemned in Larry: telling lies.

Our contingent was not scheduled to move for about an hour, so I decided to search out the Tennessee group, which luckily was nearby. "You were right," I told Chuck and Phil. "And I don't want to discuss it." We gossiped about who did and who didn't show up to march with Tennessee, and after a few minutes I said good-bye to Chuck and Phil and headed toward the safe anonymity of the Los Angeles contingent.

On the way I heard a familiar voice say, "Hey, Stuart, how's it going?" I turned to find Dan, a man I had dated for a few months in Los Angeles. His broad smile was a welcome sight in this sea of strangers.

"I'm doing OK," I replied.

I had enjoyed going out with Dan, though we lacked the chemistry necessary for anything more than a casual relationship. We had both realized that at about the same time, so our breakup hadn't been dramatic.

We ended up spending the entire day together, eventually separating from the slow-moving Los Angeles group and marching on our own. I told Dan about Larry, and he empathized. He had been there before. We held hands as we walked—enjoying each other and the day's events. That night we made love in his hotel room. I did not call Larry to tell him where I was. Dan and I have remained friends, but our lovemaking was limited to that night.

The next morning I returned to Larry's, packed my things, and left a note saying I had decided to go to Boston a few days earlier than planned. I hoped my unexplained absence the night before had left him bereft with worry, but I doubted that was the case. He had probably slept with his other boyfriend and not even missed me.

As the train chugged its way to Boston, I pondered the events of the previous week. It was strange. I was angry with Larry, but I wasn't as heartbroken as I felt I should be. I realized I had transferred my desire for family into an imaginary love for Larry. The truth was, besides a few weeks together and a batch of letters, we didn't know each other. Our relationship had been the perfect setup for someone, like me, in the midst of emotional upheaval. I could pour out my feelings in letters without responsibility for the day-to-day maintenance of a relationship. I decided I needed to find another outlet for my emotions, something positive. *A book,* I thought. The idea grabbed hold and refused to let go. I could not wait to get to Boston and tell Scott.

Scott met me at the train station. The last time I'd seen him he was a thin, boyish teenager. He had grown taller and filled out. The cute boy had become a handsome man. He grabbed my bags and hustled me to the T, Boston's subway system. We chatted easily, as if no time at all had elapsed in our friendship. It was comforting to be with someone who had known me for such a long time and who also knew my family. I wanted to pour my heart out immediately, but decided to settle in before dampening the mood.

Scott lived on Beacon Hill, which was as picturesque as I had imagined. We trekked from the T up a stunning but steep cobblestone street, and then up five flights of narrow stairs to his apartment. His building was historic and beautiful but desperately in need of an elevator—and central air-conditioning, as I soon found out.

After meeting his two female roommates and showering in the smallest bathroom in the smallest three-bedroom apartment I had ever seen, my friend and I headed out to explore Boston's gay nightlife. On our walk to a bar that featured a happy hour, Scott explained that most people in

Boston, unless they were rich, lived in cramped quarters similar to his. His rent easily exceeded mine—for less than half the space.

The crowd at the bar was sparse, which was fine with me. I wanted to hear about Scott's life since high school and was happy that he agreed to go first in the catch-up game. He had attended an Ivy League university followed by law school in Indiana, worked briefly as a "political hack," and then moved to Boston for more graduate school. He had tried to lead the life he was supposed to lead—successful lawyer like his father, then a career in politics—but discovered his true passion was writing. He had enrolled in a master's program in writing and publishing and for the first time in his life believed he was on the right track.

Scott had realized he was gay in high school and even suspected that I was, but he hadn't acted on his feelings until years later. To him, being gay was just the way it was. An intellectual, he hadn't grappled with moral or religious dilemmas as I had. He wasn't out to his family but thought they would take it in stride, just as they had accepted his decision to abandon a lucrative career in law. Unlike me, his life did not revolve around his gayness. I was envious of the ease with which he accepted himself.

By the time we finished our second beer, Scott had filled me in on ten years of his life. It was my turn to share. I knew my story would take much more time and alcohol, and I suggested we move to another bar. On the way I began my coming-out tale, allowing the pain to bubble to the surface.

I'm sure we went to several more bars that evening, but I don't remember which ones or how many. All I remember is telling Scott everything. He listened intently and seemed to understand everything I said without ever asking for clarification. It was as if he was a long-lost member of my family who knew firsthand the people and places I described, which, in point of fact, he did. He had always considered my family's religious beliefs extreme but could not believe their reaction. He couldn't understand how people who espoused the love of Christ could hate so viciously.

The next day we toured historic Boston. On our way to the harbor, to the Boston Tea Party ship, I told Scott my idea for a book. I told him about the letters from the prayer warriors and that I thought I might be able to help others experiencing religious persecution and rejection. He said, "I don't know how you've survived this, but if you're strong enough to share your story, I think you should, and I'll help you any way I can." That was all the encouragement I needed.

The week was over before I knew it. I said good-bye to Scott and headed back to Los Angeles, my spirits brighter than they had been in months. My father was right. The prayer warriors would change my life—just not in the way they had hoped—and they would help me better the lives of others too.

CHAPTER 9

NO-MAN'S-LAND

I returned to Los Angeles with a new sense of purpose. Participating in the march had allowed me to fully experience for the first time the incredible love, power, and diversity of the gay and lesbian community. My story, as important as it was to me, was simply one of the hundreds of thousands of stories that week. I had begun to understand that every step I took followed on the blood, sweat, and tears of individuals who had gone before me, who stood up for themselves and what they knew was right. Now, I decided, it was my turn to break ground. I would become an advocate for those lacking the power to speak for themselves—for Robert, for his Aunt Darlene, for the person I had been just a few months earlier.

The weeks passed quickly. The Gay and Lesbian Center provided endless distractions that kept me from beginning work on the book. Soon, however, I opened the drawer containing my photo album and the letters I had received. I spent an entire day rereading the letters and leafing through the book of pictures my mother had once said she could never part with. My life lay before me, and the pain was palpable, unbearable. I didn't know if I would be able to write about something so personal, so intimate, so revealing.

I prayed for guidance as the sunlight waned. Eventually, I fell asleep. I awoke a few hours later with a deep sense of peace and clarity. I walked to the makeshift desk in my bedroom and began to write. My story flowed from my brain to my fingers to the keyboard. By dawn, I had completed a draft of the first chapter.

As spring turned to summer, I continued to write. I felt stronger and better about my life. I was changing, growing in a way I had never imagined. Writing was therapy. It helped me let go of the past and put my family into perspective.

I did not hear from my parents after my mother's hysterical call in Washington until the beginning of June, when I received a letter from my father. He began by telling me that although his words might sound foreign to me, he was certain that one day I would be desperate to escape the "trap of homosexuality." He wrote that many men had made the change from homosexual to heterosexual. He said that when the time came for me to do so, he would supply me with the names of counselors who could help with my conversion. He wrote, "We eagerly await your return with open arms." He included a poem titled *The Porch Light*, author unknown to me, which uses the analogy of a porch light shining brightly, awaiting a son's return to home and God.

I wanted to believe that he and my mother were trying to reach out and decided to temper my response. I waited more than a week before composing and sending my letter.

June 18, 1993

Dear Dad,

I received your letter a few days ago and finally have the opportunity to sit down and write you back. I am not sure if you wrote the poem, but it was beautiful. While I do not agree with its content or feel it is representative of our relationship, I appreciate the love and sentiment it expresses.

Is the porch light really on? In my experience it is only on if I agree with your beliefs and views. It is not an unconditional porch light, but one that carries many strings and restrictions. It is your porch light and your home and your beliefs. There seems to be little or no room for any light that shines outside of your realm.

I am trying to empathize with what you and Mother are experiencing, but I must repeat that I am an adult now and am making a life for myself. Just as you did when you were my age, I am choosing the life that I believe is best for me. Your view differed from your father's, but it didn't matter. You had to make choices for yourself. If the choices you made have put you in closer communion with God, as mine have, then I commend you. I don't need to judge your choices because they are between you and God. Only God knows our hearts, and I can say that I feel better about my relationship with God than I ever have. God is an active part of my life now, not someone I ran from for so many years.

What you would have done had your father constantly judged you and told you that your values, beliefs, and lifestyle were wrong? Would your choices have been different because of his opinion? I have hoped for many years that you would love and respect me for who I am, while letting me be responsible for my own life. I respect the choices you have made, even though I do not agree with many of them. It is your life.

To me this is not just an issue of gay vs. straight, but an issue of choices. I feel you want to control and judge my choices. I am responsible for my happiness, my spiritual life, and my choices, not you. I expect you to respect my decisions if you want to be a part of my life.

I do wish you happiness and peace. May your Father's Day be filled with love and joy.

Stuart

P.S.:

• *Over 90% of all gay men who enter "rehab" programs return to a life of homosexuality.*

• *There are many Christians, clergy and laypeople, who do not hold your views regarding homosexuality. They have done exhaustive research into the historical context of the Bible and homosexuality. As an educated man, you should want all the information, not just one side. I would be happy to put you in contact with some of these individuals if you would like.*

• *There are support groups, such as Parents and Friends of Lesbians and Gays, in your area. There are several parents in Murfreesboro that would be willing to talk with you.*

• *There are Christian counselors who will not try to talk you into accepting this but who could help with some of the emotional aspects you may be dealing with. Counseling provides a safe space for you to discuss your feelings rather than your opinions or thoughts. Please look into this.*

• *Have you read the book I left you? It was written by parents with gay children.*

• *Remember, I grew up with all of your views and opinions. I have read all the literature from fundamentalist groups and feel sure that I understand the basis of your viewpoint. If you cannot meet me halfway and at least look into some of the above, then I don't see how you can say that you are in any way trying to heal our relationship. This does not have to be about either one of us being right. It can be about acceptance, respect, and tolerance.*

I hoped my letter might open a dialogue between my father and me. I still thought that someone as bright and educated as he could overcome his rabid homophobia. If he would just open up a little bit, I believed we could make headway.

I spent the next month at work preparing for the Los Angeles Gay Pride Festival and waiting for a response from my father, which didn't come. His silence was bothersome, but I had just received a promotion and raise, and the book was humming along. Things were going well. I had not heard from my family or the other prayer warriors in several months and started to believe things were finally settling down.

I returned from lunch one August afternoon, however, to a voice mail message from Aunt Brenda, asking me to call. I hit the keypad to replay the message. I had not spoken with anyone in my family for more than four months, and her voice chilled me. I harbored a ray of hope that she wanted to apologize for disowning me and had called to offer an olive branch, but the tone of her voice suggested otherwise.

I walked to Julie's office and asked if she would sit with me while I called my aunt. I wanted moral support. With Julie's hand steadying my own, I dialed the number I knew by heart. One of my cousins answered. I offered a friendly greeting and received silence in return, followed by Brenda's voice. "I was just calling to see if you were still happy," she said. I told her I was, to which she replied, "Oh, I was hoping you wouldn't be." She told me I was no longer part of her family—a fact her letter the previous year had made clear—bemoaning the fact that I had "hurt everyone deeply." The call lasted only a few minutes but left me exhausted.

I had once adored my aunt, believing that of all the people in my family, she would be the most understanding. I had wanted Brenda to be there for my mother after I came out to provide comfort and to help Mother understand that homosexuality was just another wrinkle in humanity. After all, Brenda was the woman who had chastised my mother for saying AIDS was God's way of punishing homosexuals. Now our years of friendship were gone, replaced with bitterness and bigotry.

On the phone I had wanted to tell Brenda about the several gay people she knew and adored, but who were not out to her. I had seen one of her and my uncle's friends many times at a country and western gay bar in Nashville, for example. He had asked me not to tell my family about him, though, and I had to respect his request. I wondered what effect my coming out had on him. Had Brenda and Ray shared with him the story of disowning me? Had they told him how horrible they thought being gay was? Had he listened and said nothing in my defense, in his own defense? I felt sorry for this man who lived his life in the closet, afraid of losing people he cared about like my aunt and uncle—legitimately afraid, unfortunately.

I spent the rest of the day concentrating on work, burying myself in the needs of my staff and volunteers. It was strange working for a flagship of the gay and lesbian movement, a place that stood for being out and proud, when inside I wanted to crawl under a rock and disappear. I felt like a phony. Depression set in as I realized my brave facade was exactly that—a facade.

That evening, however, another letter arrived from Linda, cheering me up. She reminded me that not everyone considered me a horrible, selfish deviant. She encouraged me to "keep my chin up." I was grateful for her kindness and vowed to push forward, no matter how bleak the future might seem.

A few days later I finally received a note from my father. He wrote of the activities my family had enjoyed over the summer but did not mention the letter I had sent in June. I found his lack of response strange and wondered why he was suddenly easing up on the prayer war. Was this another tactic, or had he decided to ignore my thoughts? Either way, I felt myself pulling further and further away from the family that had once anchored my world.

September ended my respite from the prayer warriors. The first letter in an onslaught that continues even today was from Helen, a Believers' Chapel parishioner whose children I had known while growing up. Helen was a sweet woman who always had a kind word or a smile for me.

She told me my family had given her "the liberty to write you as I would my very own," as if I were nothing more than my parent's property, chattel, subject to their whims. "The scary thing about being a parent," she wrote, "is that there are no guarantees. We strive to teach our children the truths of God's word, and we pray that they will accept Jesus as their savior and live for Him. Yet children from the most godly families have been known to reject it all." Once again, I thought, it was about the beliefs and wishes of the parents and not the child. She continued by comparing "the sin of homosexuality" to the near-tragic journey of a group of mountain climbers who almost lost their lives because of "mistaken choices," little realizing I hadn't chosen to be gay any more than her mythical mountain climbers would have chosen to hike the path of an avalanche. She closed by pleading with me to "reject the wrong but return to the right." Nowhere in her three-page letter did she ask my beliefs or opinions about Christianity. Instead, like the others, she assumed I was either a fallen Christian or not a Christian at all.

Another letter, from a doctor and his wife who didn't attend my parents' church but were members of another fundamentalist congregation in Murfreesboro, stated, "Your dad and mother have asked us to pray and write to you about your lifestyle." The letter talked about the blessings of God and about the "curses He bestows on the wicked." One unique thing about this letter was the writers' expression of their own shortcomings and struggles. The doctor and his wife made an effort to not be judgmental, though they lacked any understanding of the fact that homosexuality is not a choice.

As my 28th birthday approached, the letters continued to roll in, quashing any desire I might have had to celebrate. The constant barrage left me bitter and antisocial. Until then, I had believed my parents, or at least my mother, would eventually come around. But more than a year had passed, and things were getting worse. Knowing that the people I counted on the most had deserted me led me to question all of my relationships.

I sabotaged several friendships in order to become as unlovable as my family had convinced me I was. By mid October I had alienated my roommate, Scott, and was unable to allow a wonderful man I was dating, Chris, to get close to me. I never reached the point where I actually planned my suicide, but I wished I was dead on many occasions. I hid my feelings at work and around others who did not know me well. But I couldn't hide my emotions from those closest to me, like Scott and Chris, so I cut them out of my life. I always made it their fault, of course, traveling my own road of self-righteous denial. Luckily, I was able to repair the many relationships I damaged during this dark period. I encourage anyone who goes through a similar experience to seek professional counseling. In retrospect, I see that it would have made my life and the lives of those around me considerably easier.

On my birthday I received a card and check from my mother and father. Angry that they had not responded to the letter I had written in June, I wrote a reply.

October 20, 1993

Dear Mom and Dad,

Thank you for the birthday card. I am returning your check. As you said last Christmas, "gifts are not necessary." The only gift that I want from you is that you stop judging me and start accepting me for who I am.

As I wrote in my letter to you this summer, I do not wish to cut you out of my life. But you must be willing to meet me halfway. Until then, I really don't have anything else to say.

I know that you are hurting, and that hurts me. Things do not have to be this way. I do love you.

Take care. I am fine—financially, emotionally, and spiritually.

Stuart

A few days later I received more letters from home. My mother wrote that she sent me the money "because that is what we do for Monty and Barb, and we wanted to do the same for you." She went on to say, "by telling you we love you and that you are welcome home anytime to visit, we have met you halfway." She added that she and Dad wouldn't, of course, be able to welcome any of my gay friends. She closed by saying, "I feel that as a mother and spiritual developer, I failed. I am hurt, angry, sad, disappointed, and feel a part of my life has died."

I put the letter down and began to cry. She said that she felt like a failure, but it felt like she had said *I* was the failure. My lifetime of achievements suddenly meant nothing. My love for her meant nothing.

Another of the letters was from my oldest sister, Amy, who was about to graduate from high school. I had not heard from her since coming out and hoped she would show compassion for the brother who used to curl her hair and dress her like a Barbie doll. Those hopes were quickly dashed. She said she was "shocked, hurt, disgusted, and very angry." She called me "very selfish" and said no one was going to meet me halfway.

It was only early afternoon, but I wanted to sleep. I crawled into bed. Escape. I knew this was an obvious sign of depression, but I didn't care.

By December I had completely isolated myself. I broke up with Chris and told Scott one morning before leaving for work that I was moving out at the end of the month. He was shocked and hurt and asked if we could talk about it. I told him my mind was made up, and there was nothing to discuss. It felt like the day my father forced fundamentalism on his unsuspecting family, except from the other end; Chris and Scott reacted to my decisions with the same confusion my mother, brother, and I had reacted to my father's, but I was not to be swayed.

I found a small one-bedroom apartment in West Hollywood and retreated from the world. I spent Christmas in Palm Springs at a notoriously seedy gay resort, the perfect numbing experience for someone wanting to escape anything that even looked like a heterosexual family.

Immediately following my joyless Christmas, I received a letter from my Uncle Jere, my father's youngest brother. Jere and his wife Linda (not the same Uncle Jerry and Linda as on my mom's side) lived in the small town where my father grew up, owned an advertising company, and attended the local Methodist church. I had written them in

November to explain why I wouldn't be home for the holidays. When I didn't receive a response, I assumed they agreed with my parents' views.

Fortunately, I was wrong.

Jere apologized for not writing sooner. He told a story about an old woman in his church who continued driving long after she should have. He said he helped her every week as she pulled up to the church, sometimes stopping traffic to ensure her safety. He explained he never felt it was his place to tell others how to live and wrote, "I'm sorry your relationship with your family is strained. Don't concentrate on harsh words or reflex actions from your mother, father, sisters, brother, aunts, or uncles. Listen for the love that you know is there, and base your relationship with them on love. Love never disowned someone, and love always wants you around."

I wished Uncle Jere and Linda were my parents; they could have loved a child who was different. I wanted Uncle Jere to stand up to my father but knew this was not his style. He loved me, and he loved my father. He wanted a relationship with both of us. And I had proven that confronting my father could put an end to that.

As I prepared for a new year, I knew my life was not where it needed to be. But I could not find the strength to reach out for help. Despite Uncle Jere's supportive letter, I ended the year with my spirits at an all-time low.

C H A P T E R   1 0

WAR BONDS

June 1996

"Ladies and Gentleman, this is your captain speaking. We are currently over Little Rock, Ark., and will be arriving in Nashville in approximately one hour. The temperature in Nashville is..."

I woke abruptly from my nap, startled by the captain's booming voice, and remembered I was on yet another mission to Nashville. It had been almost four years since the ill-fated trip when I told my family I am gay. This time I was flying home to tell it to the world, or at least the portion of the world that would be attending Nashville's Gay and Lesbian Pride Festival. The organizers had heard about my experiences and forthcoming book—I had, by this time, signed a contract for publication—and asked me to serve as keynote speaker. I pictured the headline: "Local queer boy makes good." I was honored to follow in the footsteps of previous speakers like Donna Red Wing and Urvashi Vaid.

Our talkative captain clicked off his mike, and I re-closed my eyes, scrunching back into my not-so-comfortable seat. I wondered if my story would seem relevant to anyone other than me. I didn't know if anyone would care. I wasn't a national leader, and I certainly wasn't famous. I prayed that the story of a young man who lost his family but found himself would make a difference, even if only to one person. As I drifted back to sleep, my mind sifted the events of the past four years.

The beginning of 1994 was the most difficult period of my life. Cut off from those who knew me best and loved me the most, I developed a thick shell that protected me from the world. I threw myself into work and kept the few friends who were still speaking to me at a distance. I was drowning in depression. My faith was lost. I was angry at everyone, especially God. I was a walking corpse. I couldn't remember joy or happiness. At home, I sat for hours in the dark and sobbed. I had facilitated groups for years and seen the benefits of therapy, but I couldn't bring myself to get help.

I had a family, but they didn't want me.

One interesting development in an otherwise dismal spring was a trip to Tennessee to lead a weekend training session for local AIDS organizations. The training would take place in Chattanooga. I scheduled just enough time to land in Nashville, see a few friends, and then dash to Chattanooga. I had written to my grandmother to let her know I would be in Tennessee for a few days and wanted to see her. I did not, however, tell my parents about the trip. I figured they didn't want to see me, and I was in no mood to be nice to them anyway.

A few weeks before I left, I received a letter from my mother. She and my father wanted to see me, even if it meant driving two hours to Chattanooga. My grandmother, apparently, had told them about my upcoming trip.

I picked up the phone and dialed home. Abby answered and called my mother to the phone. My sister, once so close, had nothing to say to me. Mother and I exchanged pleasantries, then got to the point. "I got your letter," I said, "and was wondering why you wanted to see me."

"We'd just like to see you is all."

"Mother, I have to say, I asked you and Dad for some very specific things in a letter in July. You never responded. And when I returned the check you sent for my birthday, I asked again. Still no response. So I don't understand why you want to see me."

"Well, we've decided we want a relationship, even if it's superficial."

I asked if they had talked to a PFLAG member or seen a counselor or spoken with any theologians who didn't agree with their interpretation of the Bible or read the book I left.

"Well, I have read some books," she said, "by Beverly Johnson. And your dad has gone to see Jack Jr." (Beverly Johnson was the author of antigay fundamentalist Christian books. Jack Jr. was the openly gay son of a couple in town; meeting with my father must have been great fun for him.) Mother continued, "We asked you to go see a Christian counselor. Did you do that?"

"No," I answered. "But there's a difference. I grew up in your church, immersed in your beliefs. I understand your point of view. All I've asked of you is to extend me the same courtesy. But you won't. You haven't even read the book I left."

"I don't have it anymore. I won't read it because it's written by gay people."

"No, it was written by two mothers with gay children."

We went round and round, me arguing she should consider other points of view, she retreating to the sanctity of Bible verses.

"Your father and I are trying," she said. "We are doing the best we can, but we can't accept your lifestyle choice."

"Mother, all I ever wanted from you was compassion. You don't have to accept homosexuality, just me."

"I wish you could see what you've done to this family. Your sister Amy is sitting in the living room crying her eyes out."

I was furious. "Don't put that on me, Mother. It was your decision to fill their heads with one-sided information. What did you expect? They are little girls. They only know what you tell them."

Our conversation went downhill from there, mostly the result of my pent-up anger bursting forth. I had never directed such venom at my mother but blaming me for upsetting my sisters was more than I could take.

I did not call while in Tennessee, driving past my old hometown on the way to Chattanooga without a second glance.

The next few months passed slowly; the only bright spot on the horizon was a planned trip to Hawaii. I cooled down after the argument with my mother and sent my sister Amy a high school graduation present, offering to fly her to California for a visit. She declined but wrote a sweet thank-you note, the first kind words I had gotten from her since coming out. I also sent my mother a Mother's Day card. I was thankful for the love she had shown me as a child and figured that even an estranged mother deserves to be thanked for bringing you into the world. She wrote back, thanking me for remembering her, but not mentioning our strained relationship.

Hawaii was just what the doctor ordered. My former roommate John and I flew over to spend a week at my friend David's condo in Ka'anapali, Maui. The week was wonderful. I mended my tattered friendship with John and grew closer to David. And I surprised myself by making new friends. At a cocktail party David threw for other Los Angeles–based visitors, I met Will, an attorney and activist, and his friend Carmichael, also an attorney—men who eventually became some of my closest friends. My depression lifted, and for the first time in almost six months, I prayed, thanking God for showing me, once again, the beauty in the world.

By the end of the vacation I felt alive, rejuvenated. And while I dreaded leaving the island, I was excited at the prospect of returning to Los Angeles and rebuilding the life I had put on hold for more than a year.

The summer passed quickly. I began the process of repairing the relationships I had damaged, explored and enjoyed my new friendships, and settled in to yet another new job at the Gay and Lesbian Center. For the first time since my parents' rejection, I reached out and shared my pain, banishing my "brave face" to the closet where it belonged. Not surprisingly, my friends were incredibly supportive. I began to realize there was no shame in showing my emotions.

At the end of the summer, the management team in my department decided we should attend a weekend communications workshop called the Forum. The Forum was an offshoot of the Est movement, which had been popular in California in the '70s and '80s, and was being used in corporate environments with great success.

The first night of the workshop was difficult. The man leading the group reminded me of my father, able to win arguments by twisting logic to serve his needs. He constantly corrected people in a condescending manner that I felt was designed to break their will. I had seen such tactics used by the religious right and was appalled. At the end of the night, I told my coworkers I wouldn't be returning the next day.

They agreed it was a difficult evening but asked me to come back the next morning. After 30 minutes of discussion, I agreed but told them I would leave at the lunch break if things didn't improve.

The next morning I was in a better frame of mind. I was actually a little embarrassed by my harsh reaction the previous night. My inability to relinquish control surprised me. I wondered how much of my life was spent fleeing people who threatened my freedom.

I sat through the morning session, still bristling at the leader's technique. But I listened to the stories of people as they spoke about their problems. After a while a pattern emerged. The severity of the problems varied, but the core issue was abandonment. At some point, a trusted person had let them down, creating a well of mistrust that colored their relationships ever after. To alleviate their anguish, they created stories explaining why they had been wronged, usually sounding like self-righteous martyrs.

Did I sound that way? I thought.

I did not leave after lunch.

That afternoon the session leader asked us to make a list of all the people we felt had wronged us. We learned that the stories we created to explain why someone we loved had hurt us were not based in any reality but our own. We learned that most of the time we didn't know the real reason a person had hurt us because we never asked. We learned that we made ourselves right by making everyone else wrong.

I didn't like the messenger, but the message made sense. It was the same message I had heard from Marianne Williamson, only now I was prepared to act on it. I thought about my father and how I had spent my life perceiving him a certain way. He was the villain, and I was the victim. Always. But no story was that simple.

Near the end of the workshop, we were instructed to call the people on our list to "clean things up." The workshop had made phones available, but I feared my call would go poorly and wanted privacy. I walked across the street to a pay phone. I dialed home, hoping my mother would answer so I could start with her and then ease into a conversation with my father, who I had not spoken with in more than two years. My hands shook as the phone rang.

My father answered.

I explained that I had been attending a weekend workshop and had learned a great deal about myself. I apologized for making him wrong all my life and told him I wanted to start over.

"Praise the Lord," he said, and we both let out a nervous laugh. He thanked me for calling and said he wanted to see me. I told him I would be attending a conference in Atlanta in a few months and invited him and Mother to visit. He agreed.

In October I flew to Atlanta to present a workshop at the largest AIDS conference in the country and to see my parents for the first time since telling them I was gay. By the time the plane landed I was a nervous wreck.

My parents met me in front of my hotel a few hours after I arrived. I wasn't sure how to greet them. My mother took the lead and gave me a hug. My heart skipped a beat. We drove to a restaurant my father had selected and proceeded to have a pleasant dinner. Nothing was mentioned about my homosexuality or our estrangement. Instead, they filled me in on what was going on with the family. Two hours passed quickly, and before I knew it I was back at my hotel. We said good night and agreed to meet the next morning for coffee. They said they needed to leave right after that to be back in Murfreesboro for an afternoon church event.

We hadn't discussed anything about my life, but we had managed to spend an evening together with no arguments. I wanted to believe this was the beginning of a new relationship with my parents. In bed that night I let go of everything that had happened and prepared for a new beginning.

The next morning I rose early to meet Mom and Dad for coffee. I thanked them for a lovely evening. We chatted for a few minutes and then I said, "I was thinking I'd like to come home for Christmas this year."

After a long pause, my mother said she didn't think that would be such a good idea. A look of sadness and pain replaced her smile.

"Why not?" I asked.

"If you come home, other people won't," my father said.

I was stunned. I pressed for information, and my father finally told me that my brother, sisters, and others did not want to be around me. I was devastated.

Mother cried and told me I was the cause of it all. It was my choice to be gay, she said, and I should have known how the family would react.

As calmly as I could, I once again explained that being gay isn't a choice. It was how I was born and there was nothing I could do. I had been gay my entire life. The only difference between now and before was that now they knew about it.

My father commented on how ironic it was that he was the most supportive person in our family, that the people I had thought would be there for me had deserted me and wanted nothing to do with me.

The man whose initial reaction and subsequent behavior had fueled and fanned the flames of my family's homophobia was painting himself as my greatest ally. I thought back to the Forum. All my life, he was the villain, and I was the victim. Maybe the story really was that simple.

"Why would you allow the actions of others to dictate whether I can come home for the holidays?" I asked.

"You're being unfair," Mom cried. "You can't expect us to choose between the rest of the family and you when it was your choice that caused everything."

"If you want, we'll meet you somewhere before or after the holidays," Dad said.

I felt like a leper.

The realization hit: Nothing had changed. My parents did not accept me. I said good-bye and headed for the bathroom, which, thankfully, was empty. I splashed cold water on my face and dried it with a paper towel. I looked in the mirror—eyes red and swollen from crying—the reflection of an all-too-familiar little boy.

I returned to Los Angeles a changed man. The grip my father held on me was broken. I could now relate to him as one man does to another. He was just a person whose behavior was as good or as bad as he chose to make it. I was responsible only for myself. He and Mother would never be the parents I had hoped they would be, and I would never be the son they prayed so earnestly for. It was time to move on.

The most frightening thing about letting your family go is that suddenly you have no one to blame. You are left alone to accept and deal with your insecurities and shortcomings. I had spent a lifetime blaming my father for everything; taking responsibility for my imperfect life was not easy. The first few months after seeing my parents in Atlanta were difficult, but I refused to slip into my old pattern of denial, blame, and martyrdom.

It wasn't long before a letter arrived that tested my resolve.

My father opened by telling me about the family's Thanksgiving feast, then moved to our recent conversation. "Your mother and I were so pleased at our meeting with you in Atlanta. Two years is too long to be separated from loved ones. We find ourselves in the middle between you and the rest of the family, and it is not always a pleasant role. The Lord has given love to us for you, and we have tried to pass it along to you as best we know how given the realities. We love you very much and at the same time are extremely fearful for you. We are trusting the Lord to watch over you, to take care of you, and to woo you to Himself."

How ironic that he viewed himself as being in the middle between me and the family. If he really wanted to patch things up, he could call a family meeting and lay his cards on the table. His position was disingenuous. But it was his life. I pulled the love from his letter and ignored the rest.

My resolve had survived. I passed the test.

I have since received many more letters from my father and other prayer warriors, and I have dealt with them all in the same fashion—accepting the love, forgetting the rest. The softening of my heart had a strange effect on many of the prayer warriors. Their letters, for the most part, became more loving and less judgmental.

I realized that I would probably never have a close relationship with my family again. But I was blessed with incredible, loving friends, and I let them become the family I longed for. Relinquishing the past was not easy, but the future unfolded in many wonderful new ways. I had weathered the storm, and when I looked out the window of my soul, I saw the rains had fostered a beautiful garden.

Nashville. It rained as I made my way to the pride parade kickoff, to be followed by my speech—indoors, thankfully—at the festival.

Familiar faces dotted the crowd. Two of my dearest friends, Donna and Sue, had left their husbands in Murfreesboro and braved the rain to lend their support. I spotted them, and we slipped off to grab lunch and catch up. After tacos and gossip we drove to a nearby gay bar that housed a 1,500-seat theater, in which I would deliver my speech. Donna and Sue were amazed by the size of the bar and the crowd that packed it. This was a far cry from the first Nashville Pride I had participated in, an event that drew less than 100 people.

Before I knew it, I was called to the stage. I took a deep breath, said a quick prayer, and walked to the microphone. "My name is Stuart Howell Miller. I'm proud to be a Tennessean and even more proud to be a gay American!" I said. "I know we're here to celebrate our lives and accomplishments, but first I want to talk to you about the hard work we still have to do."

I told the story of Rebecca, a young woman I had met at the center in Los Angeles a few weeks before. She was 19 years old, tall, self-assured, with short blond hair and a beautiful smile. "When she was 11," I said, "her parents kicked her out of her Jackson, S.C., home after walking in on her kissing another girl. At age 11, she was on the street. She had no money but made her way to the train station, where she hopped a freight car with another homeless youth." I told them how Rebecca had drifted across the country, surviving any way she could, eventually making it to Los Angeles and the Gay and Lesbian Center, where she had begun to rebuild her life. I explained that we see all too many "Rebeccas" at the center because most communities provide no support to gay youth.

And then I told the audience what I had in common with Rebecca. We were both orphans, and the worst kind. Our parents were alive but didn't want us. There were many of us, I said, both old and young, who shared this common pain.

I spoke about the prayer war—about my pain, my depression, my eventual recovery. "Today," I said, "even though my family continues to fight their prayer war, I have hope, for myself and for others. My hope comes from the knowledge that I was created perfect just as I am and that you all were created perfect just as you are. And no one—not my parents, my siblings, the church, or even Pat Robertson—will make me feel differently ever again." I closed by saying, "I may not have the family I was born into, but being here today shows me that I *do* have a family. God bless you all."

Silence.

And then suddenly the crowd jumped to its feet, wildly applauding. Some in the audience wiped at tears while others yelled "Amen!" and "Praise the Lord!"

As I walked off the stage, a man grabbed my arm. "Thank you," he said. "Your story touched my heart. I hope you are OK and know that God loves you."

"Yes," I answered, "God loves us all."